LOST
SOULS

LOST SOULS

Finding Hope
in the Heart of Darkness

Niles Elliot Goldstein

BELL TOWER · NEW YORK

Grateful acknowledgment is made to the following for permission to reprint
previously published material:

HarperCollins Publishers Inc.: Poem 1 in "A Book for the Hours of Prayer" from
Selected Poems of Rainer Maria Rilke, edited and translated by Robert Bly, copyright ©
1981 by Robert Bly. Reprinted by permission of HarperCollins Publishers Inc.

Henry Holt and Company, LLC: Excerpt from "Directive" from *The Poetry of Robert Frost,*
edited by Edward Connery Lathem, copyright © 1947, 1969 by Henry Holt and Co.,
copyright renewed 1975 by Lesley Frost Ballantine. Reprinted by permission of
Henry Holt and Company, LLC.

Random House, Inc.: Excerpt from "Evening" from *The Selected Poetry of Rainer Maria Rilke,*
by Rainer Maria Rilke, translated by Stephen Mitchell, copyright © 1982 by Stephen
Mitchell. Reprinted by permission of Random House, Inc.

Published by Bell Tower, New York, New York.
Member of the Crown Publishing Group, a division of Random House, Inc.
www.randomhouse.com

Bell Tower and colophon are registered trademarks of Random House, Inc.

Printed in the United States of America

Design by Fearn Cutler De Vicq

Library of Congress Cataloging-in-Publication Data
Goldstein, Niles Elliot, 1966–
Lost souls : finding hope in the heart of darkness / Niles Elliot Goldstein.— 1st ed.
1. Suffering—Religious aspects—Judaism. 2. Life change events—Religious aspects—
Judaism. 3. Life change events—Psychological aspects. 4. Adjustment (Psychology)—
Religious aspects—Judaism. 5. Self-actualization (Psychology)
6. Judaism—Psychology. I. Title.
BM645.S9 G55 2002
296.7—dc21   2002002992

ISBN 0-609-61037-6

10 9 8 7 6 5 4 3 2 1

FIRST EDITION

For the women, men, and children
of my spiritual community, The New Shul,
who have given me more in three years
than I could give them in a lifetime

CONTENTS

Introduction   9

ONE: Disorientation   17

TWO: Panic   41

THREE: Loneliness   65

FOUR: Yearning   85

FIVE: Anger   109

SIX: Determination   133

SEVEN: Surrender   157

EIGHT: Emergence   179

Conclusion   199

Acknowledgments   203

INTRODUCTION

O URS IS AN AGE OF AGITATION AND ISOLATION. Many of us feel utterly lost as we search for purpose, community, love, even self. Some people try to deal with this sense of bewilderment, the dark woods within which we eat and sleep and live and die, through denial: We indulge in a multiplicity of diversions (such as alcohol and drugs, sex, recreation, and entertainment) to distract us from our problems or to fill the emptiness in our lives. Others seek escape through nostalgic memories of former times or grand visions of the future.

If the generation of the twenties was lost, and that of the fifties was beat, then the current one—the generation of the new millennium—is simply bewildered. We are lost *and* burned out. While modernism and modernity were supposed to have grounded, even saved us, to have given us beauty, direction, and purpose, they have proven to be false gods. The Fitzgeralds and Hemingways of the Lost Generation cracked under the weight of their excesses and the influence of alcohol; the hunger for free expression and individualism that motivated the Beat Generation devoured some of its most towering personalities. Yet at the core of both experiments was a quest for meaning. Now, however, after so many disappointments and such deep ruination, many of us seem to have abandoned that pursuit. And to have given up hope.

We have become like the animals in Martin Seligman's famous experiments on "learned helplessness." In the psychologist's research, laboratory dogs were taught that they would receive an electric shock no matter what they did (such as moving to a different part of the cage). The result was that the dogs stopped *all* action—they just sat still and accepted the shocks, as if the shocks were unavoidable, almost necessary features of their living conditions. In our own culture, many of the great ideologies, institutions, and role models our forebears embraced have either been discredited or have collapsed. The media bombards us with troubling, sometimes horrifying images that eclipse any good we witness in our daily lives. Nothing seems to have solid footing. If postmodern humanity appears dazed, confused, and immobilized in a seemingly expanding wasteland, much of its paralysis comes from the feeling that anything positive we do will inevitably be met with negative reinforcement.

Although there have been many recent books on coping with personal loss, scant attention has been paid to the phenomenon of *being* lost, of becoming a wanderer, a soul unable to find its way. This experience has nothing to do with losing external possessions; it stems from a loss that is internal. When we lose our bearings, and the reasons for this can be many and varied, some aspect of our inner machinery breaks down, gets corrupted, spirals out of control—and we find ourselves in a state of disorientation. This is a far more frightening situation than losing a job or even a relationship: What we lose is our entire world. No wonder so many of us retreat into realms of denial or fantasy rather than trying to confront the situation head on.

A soul is not doomed just because it becomes lost. Sometimes being lost is itself a catalyst for renewal and redemption. At the outset of *The Divine Comedy,* Dante, at the midpoint of his life, is aware that he has somehow strayed into a wilderness, and that the safe and familiar path he had been on is gone. Despite his fears, the poet ventures through the circles of hell, climbs the mountain of purgatory, and ultimately gains a vision of celestial paradise. In the book of Exodus, we find another illustration of how a journey through forbidding terrain can result in revelation. After passing through the crucible of their enslavement in Egypt, the Israelites roam the desert wastes of Sinai. They long for the fleshpots of their romanticized former "home." Yet it is precisely in this bleak environment that God appears to them and reveals the sacred covenant through which they and their descendants will be redeemed.

These episodes are not just epic tales but metaphors for conditions that can lead to transcendent experience. They are promises that beyond our trials and struggles there is hope, a path out of the maze that is tortuous but true. Anyone who has ever tried to travel through an open sea, a dense forest, or a vast desert knows how easy it is to become confused. History is filled with dramatic examples of men and women who lost their way. Some eventually made it out of the labyrinth. Ernest Shackleton and the crew of the *Endurance* survived a harrowing shipwreck in Antarctica and returned to England. Several members of a Paraguayan rugby team lived through a plane crash that stranded them high in the Andes by eating the flesh of those who had perished before them. But some lost souls never made it out. Robert Scott's race to the South Pole ended in his death. Amelia Earhart's transcontinental flight led not to glory but catastrophe.

We can become lost not just in body but in mind. Like many other New Yorkers, I saw the collapse of the World Trade Center on September 11, 2001. I was woken up that morning by a call from a friend, who told me that airplanes had crashed into the towers. At first, I thought she was kidding. But as I shook the sleep from my eyes, I walked out onto my Brooklyn fire escape and stared across the East River. Smoke billowed at an angle into the sky from the tops of the towers. The sight was surreal. I ran back into my apartment and turned on the television. People were fleeing from lower Manhattan, racing across the Brooklyn Bridge. There was talk of terrorism. No one seemed to know for sure what exactly was going on. Then the towers crumbled, one at a time, like columns of matchsticks. As I stood on my fire escape in absolute amazement, a shroud of smoke and ash soon enveloped the entire lower part of the island. The whole city was in a state of shock and perplexity. How could we comprehend the magnitude and implications of what we had just witnessed? How could thousands of souls vanish from the face of the earth at the same moment? How could something like this ever have happened? These unsettling questions were more than the human brain could fathom.

There are an unlimited number of contexts that can bewilder us. While the specific outcome of a journey into the wilderness (whether geographical, emotional, or existential) varies, there does seem to be a strong quality of consistency in the *stages* that we go through when we get lost. From disorientation, to yearning, to ultimate emergence, this book explores those and other stages, drawing on the lives and experiences of those of us living today as well as figures from the Bible and history. Not everybody will undergo each one of these stages, or encounter them in an identical sequence. That is because we have different personalities and unique paths. But all of us will experience some of them. We are not the first generation to feel lost, and we certainly won't be the last. Yet there is hope. We can learn from the past—and from each other. *Lost Souls* isn't a road map to salvation but, rather, a guide to a deeper understanding of the challenges of being human, a candle in a corridor of shadows.

HANNAH: I can help you because I've been through what you are going through now. I had something like your spook—I just had a different name for him. I called him the blue devil, and . . . oh . . . we had quite a battle, quite a contest between us.

SHANNON: Which you obviously won.

HANNAH: I couldn't afford to lose.

SHANNON: How'd you beat your blue devil?

HANNAH: I showed him that I could endure him and I made him respect my endurance.

TENNESSEE WILLIAMS, The Night of the Iguana

LOST SOULS

ONE DISORIENTATION

The sky puts on the darkening blue coat
held for it by a row of ancient trees;
you watch: and the lands grow distant in your sight,
one journeying to heaven, one that falls; . . .

and leave you (inexpressibly to unravel)
your life, with its immensity and fear,
so that, now bounded, now immeasurable,
it is alternately stone in you and star.

RAINER MARIA RILKE, "Evening"

THE HERD OF CARIBOU SEEMED TO STAND FIFTY FEET TALL at the shoulder, towering over the tundra like mammoths from a lost epoch. Behind it were the ragged mountains of the Brooks Range, their peaks dusted with snow from a recent storm and hammered as flat as anvils. And on the other side of the mountains, to the south, was the start of the North American continent, a vast, unbroken expanse teeming with rivers, forests, and wildlife.

I turned to face the north. The union of the midnight sun and arctic temperatures created the fata morgana, mirages that made objects even at a great distance appear enormous and exaggerated. Before me was the Beaufort Sea, part of the Arctic Ocean. At the horizon, looming like a gigantic white fortress, was the beginning of the polar ice cap, the very roof of the world. It seemed as if it were about to crash down on top of me.

I was standing on Icy Reef, a band of small islands almost three hundred miles north of the Arctic Circle that forms a fragile barrier between the Alaskan mainland and the frigid sea above it. The reef itself is just a strip of exposed rocks, gravel, and sand, no more than twenty yards in width and barely above the water line. There were logs all around me, spit out into the treeless region via river drainages from the interior's boreal forests. Smoothed by the currents and bleached by the near-incessant sun, they blanketed the shore with what looked like shards of bone.

At certain points along the reef, not more than a mile or so separated what were in essence two radically different worlds. To the south was a panorama of color—mountains, tundra, wild flowers, and animals on the mainland. To the north, nothing but the stark monochrome of the Arctic Ocean, dappled by jagged chunks of white ice that had broken off from the summer ice pack not far away. I could *feel* the powerful tension in these extreme contrasts. If I turned in one direction, I faced a great land bursting with vitality. If I shifted toward the other, I confronted a seemingly endless abyss of gray. It was as if, without flimsy Icy Reef standing guard between the two, these worlds would violently collide with each other, a cataclysm of south and north, earth and ice, movement and stasis that might set off a chain reaction that could destroy the entire cosmos.

It wasn't just a sensory overload—it was an existential one, too. For me, the reef became a metaphor for the human condition. I may have been standing on a sliver of silt, but I also straddled the cradle and the grave. The overwhelming images and optical illusions brought me to the limits of my faculties of perception, but it was awareness of the paradox of my own existence—a paradox that took concrete form in the environ-

ment surrounding me—that carried me to the terminus of
rational comprehension. I had reached the Borderline, the murky
boundary between life and death.

I became confused, disoriented. A jumble of questions
crammed my brain, queries that the sea and sky did not, or would
not, answer:

> *Who am I?*
> *What am I doing?*
> *Where am I going?*

As remote and inaccessible a location as Icy Reef was, I
understood exactly where I was on the globe. What I no longer
knew was my place in creation.

THAT FEELING OF BEING LOST on the most basic level is one that
seeps into all of us at some point in our lives. It transcends place
and time, culture and history. Artists and thinkers have tried
to capture this phenomenon, sometimes in moments of soul-
searching and sometimes in bursts of inspiration. One of Gauguin's
masterpieces is entitled *Where Do We Come From? What Are We?
Where Are We Going?* It is an enormous image of a kind of Poly-
nesian Eden, filled with figures in various states and stages of life.
It was painted, according to the artist, before he attempted suicide in 1897. The connection that Gauguin seemed to make
between the often-disorienting nature of human life and nihilis-
tic despair is clear.

Spiritual thinkers also ask the kinds of questions that can
drive some of us to self-destruction. In one of the classic texts
of rabbinic literature, *The Sayings of the Fathers,* we find the following: "Where have you come from? Where are you going?

Before whom will you have to give an accounting?" The answers that Akavia ben Mahalalel offers are designed to lead us toward humility and away from sin, but the very fact that these unsettling questions are raised suggests how essential they are to our inner lives. Not only do we have a right to these questions—we *need* them. To stretch our minds, expand our horizons, and enlarge our souls.

Many of the most important figures in the Bible ask themselves the wheres, whats, and whys of human existence. The triggers for their questions, and the roots of their bewilderment, are many and varied. Some people become lost as a result of their misdeeds, their straying from any sense of a moral compass. One of the great and tragic tales in the Torah involves Cain and Abel, the first two children of Adam and Eve. Before culture, before civilization, there was only the battle for subsistence. Cain, the first child, is a farmer, "a tiller of the ground." (Genesis 4:2) Abel is a shepherd. In a seminal act of religious expression, the brothers present offerings to God: Cain offers a gift of fruit, Abel the firstlings of his flock.

God rejects Cain's offering and accepts Abel's. Many contemporary readers of the Bible have been perplexed, even angered, by this episode. Why would God do such a thing? Why would the Creator of humanity set up a situation so pregnant with potential for jealousy and violence between siblings? For some commentators, the answer can be found in the story itself, when God says to Cain, "Why has your face fallen? If you act rightly, will it not be lifted up? But if you do not act rightly, sin crouches at the door, and you are that which it craves. Yet you may conquer it." (4:6–7) God seems to intuit the dark heart that lurks within creation's first son, the homicidal impulse that is about to erupt east of Eden.

At least, that is the standard explanation as to why God chooses the offering of one son over that of the other. And as an apology for Scripture, it works: Since Cain hasn't mastered his baser emotions, the rejection of his gift to the Almighty becomes *his* fault, not God's. Soon after this divine rejection, Cain exchanges words with Abel. We don't know what is said between them, but immediately afterward Cain murders his brother in a field. When God inquires into the whereabouts of Abel, Cain asks his infamous question: "Am I my brother's keeper?" (4:9)

Again, the standard interpretation of this question places full responsibility on Cain and completely exonerates God of any accountability. Cain's retort is usually viewed as sarcastic, implying that he understands all too well that what he did was wrong and that he is trying to hide his guilt. But there is another way to interpret this question, one that views it as an expression of genuine confusion. Perhaps Cain is really asking, *Am* I my brother's keeper? Far from being sarcastic, he is truly bewildered about his role in the world and the way he is supposed to relate to others, particularly to those in his own bloodline. This take on the classic story of sibling rivalry makes it much more complicated than it appears on the surface, and in some ways is more true to the human experience. With this reading, Cain does not break the moral code; he isn't even aware that there *is* one. His question is less an expression of sarcasm and defensiveness than one of heartfelt confusion, dismay, even pain. Cain is still a killer, a young man who veers out of control. But his heinous crime should be seen as the end result of a series of events in which God plays a role as well.

Most of us, it is probably reasonable to claim, agree that murder—the killing of innocents—is wrong. But what about all of the other, murkier moral dilemmas that arise in our lives? And

what did people do before civilization, before the moral abso-
lutes revealed at Mount Sinai? Does Cain lose his moral compass,
or is he never given one? Is God as much at fault as Cain is? As
all of us know, there are times in our lives when we feel lost in
this way, in desperate need of divine guidance.

God punishes Cain for his actions. The "tiller of the ground,"
a man rooted in his own land, is condemned to wander the
earth. Rather than bringing life out of the soil, Cain deposits into
it death and decay and will no longer reap its bounty. Yet even in
the punishment there is a kernel of compassion. God places a
mark on Cain to protect him from those who might seek his
destruction. Is it out of guilt, or merely part of some mysterious
master plan? In another twist of tragic irony, Abel, the nomadic
herdsman, finds his permanent resting place—much as the sed-
entary Cain has now been cast into an existential wilderness.
Everything about this episode suggests tensions and ironies, perplexity and disarray. Though there is a moral order, as well as a
personal responsibility we all share for others, it may be up to us
to discern just what it is. And while redemption will come, it
may not arrive until our long and circuitous journey into the
night nears its conclusion.

———

EVEN WHEN WE DO POSSESS a clear moral tradition, there are
still times when we lose our way. Take the famous case of David
and Bathsheba. Saul has passed on, and David now sits on the
throne in Jerusalem. The Israelites are at war with the Am-
monites (and their Aramean mercenaries), but King David tarries
in the capital. One day at dusk, while walking on the roof of his
palace, David catches sight of a beautiful woman bathing. After
finding out that she is Bathsheba, the wife of Uriah the Hittite

(one of the king's loyal captains), David nevertheless dispatches one of his servants to bring her into his bedchamber. After he has his way with her, he sends her back to her house. Soon after this incident, Bathsheba sends him a simple message: "I am with child." (II Samuel 11:5)

David orders her husband, Uriah, back from the front and asks him how the war is faring. The king then tells him to go back to his home and his wife for some well-deserved rest and recreation. David even presents him with a gift of food for the amorous evening he hopes Uriah will have with Bathsheba. What better way to transfer the responsibility for the child than by having her husband immediately sleep with her? But in an act of moral rectitude that stands in pointed contrast to David's sly manipulations, Uriah refuses and sleeps instead at the door of David's palace along with the rest of the king's servants. When David asks him why he didn't go home, Uriah tells him that in good conscience he *could* not, at least not while his fellow soldiers and officers are sleeping in tents in the open field, fighting for their lives. In response, and in yet another immoral machination, David informs him that he will let him return to the war zone the following day—after they feast and drink together that night. The king succeeds in getting Uriah drunk but not in getting him to stagger into his wife's bed.

So Uriah goes off to the front the next morning, but not before David gives him a note for Joab, his commander. The message orders Joab to station Uriah directly in harm's way, in the center of the "hottest" fight he can find. Joab follows the king's order, and Uriah the Hittite, loyal and valiant to the end, perishes in battle. David transforms Uriah into the messenger of his own death, orchestrating a cold and calculated murder—and through that crime David breaks one of the Ten Commandments that God

gave to his ancestors generations earlier. The king is now free to
take Bathsheba as his own wife, and she soon bears him a son.

Clearly, David has lost his way. His lust for Bathsheba, and
the "problem" that results from it, plunge him into a state of
moral and spiritual darkness. Yet it is a darkness he is not even
aware of. God sends the prophet Nathan to confront the king,
and he offers the following parable to him:

> There were two men in one city: the one rich and the
> other poor. The rich man had many flocks and herds; the
> poor man had nothing except one little ewe lamb, which
> he had acquired and reared. It had grown up together with
> him and with his children, and it ate of his food, and drank
> of his own cup, and lay in his bosom, and was like a daugh-
> ter to him. And a traveler came to the rich man, and instead
> of taking an animal from his own flocks and herds to prepare
> a meal for the wayfarer, he took the poor man's lamb and
> prepared it for the man. (12:1–4)

David is incensed by the story and calls for the rich man's
death. He demands to know exactly *who* this person is, the man
who would dare to be so cruel to someone less fortunate. The
fact that David is so oblivious as to the identity of the real sinner
to whom Nathan is not-so-subtly alluding demonstrates the
degree of his moral confusion. Cain asks God whether or not he
is his brother's keeper—at least if one reads the tale in a somewhat sympathetic way—because he was given no moral guide-
lines to follow. David has no such excuse. He is the king of the
people of Israel, bound at Sinai many years before by an eternal
covenant with God. And one of the clearest and most important
parts of that covenant is the command not to murder.

It is interesting to note that the word *disorientation* is linked etymologically to the word *orient,* understood by many to refer to Jerusalem—the very same sacred city over which David rules. To become disoriented, to become lost, means, in a certain sense, to lose one's spiritual center, one's inner grounding. This is what has happened to David, and it has happened not in a dark forest or a remote land but in the middle of the holy city itself. David has a moral compass, but he ignores it; he can recognize neither himself nor his crime in the prophet's words.

In answer to David's question, Nathan responds: "You are the man." (12:7) When confronted with this hard truth, his period of disorientation ends, and he confesses to the prophet that "I have sinned against God." (12:13) David and Bathsheba's son dies, but she bears him another son, Solomon. It is probably no accident that Solomon, known for his great wisdom, is the product of *reorientation,* a regaining of moral and spiritual footing on the part of David. It is also most likely no accident that the messianic line is traditionally ascribed to the house of David, a house that this episode makes clear is far from the model of virtue and holiness. Yet the Bible seems to be teaching us that we don't need to be saints in order to be spiritual people, or to do good work.

Franklin Delano Roosevelt was committed to social justice, the Reverend Dr. Martin Luther King to civil rights—yet both of these men were adulterers. Malcolm X was a pimp and a criminal before devoting his life to improving the lot of his people. Gauguin abandoned his family to move to Tahiti and leave the world his artistic legacy. All of these men strayed from their moral grounding but gave posterity the gifts of their talents. Whether or not they were "great" individuals or lost souls depends on which arena we evaluate them in. Perhaps they were both.

Rabbi Menachem Mendel of Kotsk, an important and fascinating hasidic thinker, comments on a verse from the book of Exodus (22:30) in which God tells the Israelites that they must be "holy men." The Kotsker Rebbe (as he is known to his followers) interprets this to mean that God does not want us to strive for a standard of morality and holiness that we will never be able to attain—God has no shortage of angels in heaven to fill that role. What God wants is for us to be holy *people,* human, fallible, imperfect. That is the goal of mortal life. When we fall short of it, when we lose our bearings or even ourselves, all we need do is get up and try again.

———

YET THERE ARE TIMES when we become lost, not because of our misdeeds but through the actions of others. I have a friend and colleague, Elizabeth, someone I have worked with on various retreats and other spiritual projects, who went through an experience that was so profound it transformed her life. Elizabeth is one of the more spiritually evolved people I know, a person who has worked for many years to strengthen her inner life and her relationship with God. I hate to admit it, but I am sometimes jealous of her: She always seems to have such great equanimity of soul, while I often feel restless in my own spiritual life. I have envied her clarity of purpose, and I long assumed that the focus she had in her internal life was the result of never having been lost. That was until she told me about the shooting.

It happened in 1990. Elizabeth was living in Nashua, New Hampshire, working as a massage therapist. Late one afternoon, after the office had closed, a disheveled man suddenly appeared in the hallway and said he wanted an appointment. Through the locked glass door, Elizabeth told him that they were closed and that he could call and make an appointment for the following week. But the man wouldn't leave. He said he didn't have a telephone. After several minutes of conversation, Elizabeth thought that if she gave the man her business card he might finally go away. She unlocked the door. The man (she says he looked "sleazy, fat, and shaking scared") then asked her to write down his name. Elizabeth turned away from him for an instant to get her appointment book, but something made her turn back. When she did, the man had a gun pointed at her chest.

It didn't seem real—she couldn't believe what was happening. Her brain struggled for meaning, for some understanding of the event. *Why do I have to go through this?* she asked herself. Then she started to get angry. *I will not let this happen to me,* she told herself. The man waved the gun at her and ordered her to back up. "No!" Elizabeth shouted. "You get out of here!" In a rage, she tried to push him out the door. Her ninety-five pounds were no match for a man who weighed well over two hundred. He closed the door behind them and tossed her aside. The man said that he wanted money, that he had just been released from prison and wasn't afraid to use the gun. Elizabeth still couldn't believe that he would actually shoot her, still strained to make sense of what was taking place. *Oh my God, why is this happening? What is the lesson here?*

The man forced her to walk further into the office, to the massage room, where her client Lisa was putting on her shoes and getting ready to go home.

"I'm sorry, Lisa, I'm so sorry," Elizabeth said. Lisa just stared at the two of them in disbelief.

"What do you want?" asked Lisa. "We'll give you anything you want." Lisa picked up her purse and emptied its contents onto the floor. Since her anger was not helping them to get out of the situation, Elizabeth decided to do the same and headed for the closet to get her pocketbook.

"No!" the man yelled. And then he said coldly: "Lie on the floor and put your hands behind your head."

The two terrified women prostrated themselves, their faces pressing into the plush rug. What followed was an excruciating silence. Then Elizabeth heard four loud bangs. The rest is a blur. The next thing she can remember is sitting up and seeing blood on her hand. It was deep red, almost hot. It took her a few moments before she realized that the blood, now all over her body, was streaming from her head.

Disorientation, mingled with grief and then rage, took hold of Elizabeth's soul from the instant she woke from the surgery to extract bullet fragments from the inside of her skull. (She survived the shooting primarily because the bullet had pierced her skull but had not entered her brain.) She couldn't understand why a strange man she had never met would want to *kill* her. She asked herself that question over and over again. *Why? Why me?* Though all of her friends told her not to search for meaning in this random event, Elizabeth couldn't help it. As she sought an answer, the sensation of falling began to overwhelm her. The violence of the episode had shattered not just her skull but her feeling of security. She felt as if no one else around her could grasp the full depth of her bewilderment.

Eventually, she started to return to the world. One of the things that helped were the bouquets of flowers that friends had sent her at the hospital in the days and weeks after the shooting. She received more than ninety of them. "Each bouquet," Elizabeth recalls, "became a measure of connection to the world I used to know. Each blossom became the tangible evidence of a person's hope and concern for me." She began to feel a "net" again, a vague sense that despite her disorientation she would not fall entirely into an abyss of insecurity and incoherence. But Elizabeth's journey into the shadows wasn't over. During the two years after the incident, she still broke into tears daily, sometimes even hourly. She would often sit and stare at the ceiling, numb to her surroundings. And then she had an affair that led to the termination of her marriage.

She had broken the heart of the man she had loved. Guilt now merged with her grief and pain. At thirty-two, Elizabeth had lost her innocence—about others and about herself. Her yearning to feel safe again was interconnected with the issue of trust, the trust in herself that she had just wiped out. "The shooting and my divorce caused a kind of psychic tearing apart," she says. "The choice seemed clear: I could go into the dismembering vortex of the underworld and try with all my might to put myself back together. Or I could let it destroy me." Elizabeth decided to sit with her pain, her grief, her feelings of moral failure. She began drawing mandalas in what she now thinks was an unconscious attempt to re-create a center after it had been annihilated. "Eventually," she says, "I discovered that what had felt like total disintegration was, in actuality, movement toward reconnection. It was the fall into the void and my willingness to stay present there that led to a stronger faith."

In the larger framework of Elizabeth's life, the shooting (and the trauma following it) took on new meaning. It became a kind of initiatory experience, a rite of passage in her personal mythology. Only the power of myth, of a living sense of the sacred, can change demons into angels, trauma into transformation. Though her friends continued to urge her not to look for meaning in what had happened to her, Elizabeth believed that *not* to seek insight from the incident would have driven her mad—even if that understanding made sense to no one else. While her journey took place in darkness rather than light, it wove her imperfections, injuries, and injustices into a tapestry that has helped to heal her. The shooting is now a vital component of Elizabeth's life, a reference point. It has become a myth and a mystery that sustains and nourishes her soul.

————

IMMORAL, SOMETIMES DESTRUCTIVE BEHAVIOR—regardless of whether it is performed *by* us or *to* us—can plunge us into a spiritual wilderness. So can despair itself. The world around us is filled with examples of difficult experiences: a couple losing their child in an accident, a middle-aged man's career suddenly ending because of a recession, a single mother losing her savings in a troubled stock market. And some of the events that lead to despair occur no matter what we do, and seem to be built into the very fabric of what it means to be human: experiencing the decline and death of one's parents, going through menopause, growing older.

In chapter 28 of the book of Genesis, the patriarch Jacob is in a state of despair. Similar to the earlier siblings Cain and Abel, Jacob and his twin brother, Esau, have been in a condition of conflict since the (literal) moment they were born, when Jacob emerges from Rebecca's womb clutching the heel of his older brother. In a ploy consistent with that image of birth, the young Jacob first steals Esau's birthright by making him sell it to him in exchange for food, then snatches their dying father Isaac's blessing from him by tricking Isaac into thinking that Jacob is really Esau. This sets the stage for a blood feud between the brothers. Esau vows to kill his younger sibling. Word is conveyed to Rebecca of her elder son's intentions, and she warns Jacob that his life is in mortal danger. She then tells Isaac to send Jacob off to find a wife in the land of Paddan-aram.

Jacob hits rock bottom. Whether it is out of fear, guilt, or the trauma of having to leave his family and birthplace, Jacob's soul finds itself—or rather *loses* itself—in a place of despair. He ventures into the unknown, his road home blocked not just by the threat to his life but by his own turbulent emotions. His only companion is the silent desert. Jacob is about to undergo a dark night of the soul. What happens next is familiar to many of us:

> And Jacob left Beersheba, and set out for Haran. And he stopped at a certain place, and remained there all night, because the sun had set; and he took one of the stones of the place, and put it under his head, and lay down in that place to sleep. And he dreamed, and a ladder was set on the ground, and the top of it reached to heaven; and angels of God were ascending and descending on it. . . . And Jacob awoke from his sleep, and he said, "Surely God is in this place, and I did not know it!" And he was shaken, and said "How full of awe is this place! This is none other than the house of God, and this is the gate to heaven!" (28:10–12, 16–17)

Exhausted in a lonely place where long shadows have melted into dusk, Jacob uses a stone as his pillow. What more powerful an image could the Torah have chosen to convey the lowly state of his inner life? When Jacob is jolted back to his normal consciousness, he has an epiphany—he now realizes that, despite his despair, confusion, and ignorance, God has been with him. What exactly is it that Jacob experiences? A dream? A vision? A hallucination? It doesn't really matter whether this episode is the result of a divine puncture into the world of the mundane, or merely a projection of some feeling or impulse within the patriarch's tortured soul. What does matter is that our spiritual center can be found even when we wander in the inner wilderness, in a place of existential uncertainty.

As one rabbinic thinker writes, commenting on Jacob's exclamation of ignorance, a human being discovers God "only when he is infused by 'I don't know,' when he himself knows that he does not know and does not pretend to have wisdom and insight." The key to this whole episode is the stone. At first, the stone serves as a symbol for Jacob's despair and disorientation. Yet after he has awakened to a higher level of consciousness, Jacob takes that same stone from under his head and places it on the earth as a pillar, anointing it with a cruse of oil and declaring his resting place holy ground. The symbol of his spiritual confusion, brought on by his inner struggle, is transformed into one of faith and reorientation. He is ready to continue his journey. The "gate of heaven," the first stage of the path toward redemption, is disorienting indeed. It is a vision of divinity whose catalyst is sometimes a nightmare.

In the biblical book of Ecclesiastes, the author despairs as he ponders the meaning and mystery of the human condition. His famous first words, "Vanity of vanities, says Kohelet; / Vanity of vanities, all is vanity" (1:2), have become a kind of mantra to many men and women over the ages who have reflected on human existence and wondered whether any of their actions ever made much of a difference, whether life had any real point, or whether there was a life beyond this one. The fact that "The sun also rises, / And the sun sinks" (1:5), that "All the rivers run into the sea, / Yet the sea is not full" (1:7), that "There is nothing new under the sun" (1:9) are all ruminations that have led some, Kohelet included, to emotional despair and mental exhaustion. Long before Hemingway and the Lost Generation, before Kerouac and the Beats, before those of us living today, there was a brooding Jew in Jerusalem named Kohelet who was just as world-weary.

Kohelet was a perplexed man. The twelve chapters that comprise his book seem to be filled with as many questions as answers or statements. It is not a narrative work, such as the books of Genesis or Exodus (which are made up of epic stories). It is not a prescriptive work, either, such as the book of Leviticus (which consists largely of rules and laws). And it is not really a prophetic, ethical work, such as the books of Amos or Hosea (which are about the moral failings of the Israelites and the ideal behavior they ought to embody). It is a manual of uncertainty, a book for those who wrestle with the complexities and paradoxes of what it means to be human, who search for some footing or foundation to prevent them from sliding deep into a void.

The awareness that existence is a synthesis of life and death, that at each and every moment all human beings are simultaneously living and dying, is a disorienting, sometimes disquieting one. It is what I experienced at Icy Reef, and it is an awareness that strikes all of us at one time or another in our lives. One way to approach existence, then, is with fear and trembling. But it shouldn't stop there. The challenge for us, as it was two millennia ago for Kohelet, is to convert that dread into something else, something sacred. Many modern writers and thinkers (such as Kafka, Camus, and Sartre) confronted this paradox with honesty but concluded that, in the end, all we are left with is absurdity, despair, tragedy. In a sense, they recoiled from the mystery. Spiritual thinkers and writers *embrace* it, arguing that despite life's paradoxes and hardships we should still rejoice in the world and its bounty.

Whether we approach our life with dread, or welcome it

with joy, depends a great deal on whether or not we think life has meaning. For a large number of the modern existentialists, it doesn't. For Kohelet, for Job (whose life and thought we will examine later), and for other important biblical and religious figures, life *does* possess meaning—though it is known to us only imperfectly. Kohelet never claims to have completely fathomed the meaning of life. Job never justifies suffering from the human perspective. Yet both men are able to cultivate a reverence for the mystery and miracle of life, as well as a capacity to celebrate it, without ignoring or dismissing the paradoxes and contradictions that inhere in it. That ability, for me, is one of the most lasting and relevant legacies of biblical wisdom. And one of the most courageous.

———

SOMETIMES, because of our desire for stability and consistency, we become too attached to persons or things. When that happens, and when they elude or abandon us, our souls can spin out of control and leave us feeling lost. Human beings can become so identified with that which is external that at times we can lose our very sense of self—or, in extreme circumstances, even our will to live—if the bond is severed. A woman I know, Heather, went through that kind of experience. Heather grew up in a strict fundamentalist Christian household in the Denver area. She never dated, had a rigid curfew, and until she went to college at eighteen, rarely left her town or family. Heather married the first man who held her hand. She met him in school, and they were engaged by the time she was twenty. A few years later, Heather had two daughters and was living a conventional fundamentalist lifestyle in Denver. Her place and role were clear: Her job was to raise her kids and support her husband. Everything seemed fine. Comfortable. Orderly.

But then Heather found out that her fundamentalist Christian husband was having an affair with her best friend. Unable to trust him any longer, and unwilling to be married to a man who had so blatantly betrayed her, she filed for divorce. Within a short period of time, Heather's entire world had collapsed. Her whole life had been governed and guided by the religious rules and spiritual values she thought her husband embodied. When he failed her, it was as if her very faith had let her down. Not only was Heather now a single Christian woman trying to raise two girls and find a profession—she was a person cut adrift from the moorings that had made her feel so safe and secure. Her entire identity had been entwined with a man and a community she no longer trusted. Heather wasn't certain what to do next. She wasn't even sure who she was anymore.

Part of what Heather experienced was anger. And rebellion seemed to be as good a path as any to lash out at the forces that abandoned her. She turned her back on many of the religious commitments that had formerly grounded her. She began looking into other faith traditions and started dating an atheist. Yet after some time, Heather grew weary of doing battle against her hobgoblins. She realized that the failings of one man were not necessarily linked to the community that produced him. And she gradually understood that she was at fault as well, for allowing her sense of self to become inseparable from and entangled with another person. These realizations, she says, made her a stronger and wiser human being. They also helped to bring her back to her center again, to return to the heritage and community that had earlier given her such sustenance. Heather doesn't regret what happened to her. She views the chaos and confusion she was forced to work through as her passage into womanhood and maturity.

We don't always form excessive attachments to other people.

Sometimes we bond our identities to *things*. For some, that might be a title or an office, such as a CEO, a physician, or an editor. For others, it might be wealth or power. Whatever it is, if we tie our self-consciousness or self-worth to externals, and if we then lose them, our psyches can be devastated. One of the best-known figures from the book of Judges is Samson. While he is still in his mother's womb, Samson is consecrated as a Nazir, a special class of ancient Israelites committed to various ascetic disciplines, particularly abstention from wine and the refusal to cut their hair. Historically, the Nazir functioned as a member of a religious subgroup within the Jewish community of that period. Unlike the priest or the Levite, whose group membership was based on heredity, the Nazir generally *chose* his spiritual vocation; there was nothing supernatural about it. Samson is different both because his Nazirite vows were made for him and because those vows led, according to legend, to superhuman strength.

At the time, the Israelites were under the domination of the Philistines, a powerful people who were concentrated along the Mediterranean coast. Samson, as a young man, begins to stir up trouble against them, killing hundreds in retribution for various injustices. He becomes a judge, a charismatic leader, to his people for twenty years. Yet Samson eventually falls in love with a woman, Delilah, who is allied with the Philistines. They bribe her to find out how to vanquish the Jewish strongman. Samson's attachment to Delilah is deep, and even after she tries three separate times to discover the true source of his strength, Samson is blind to her manipulations and hidden agenda. Because he is also attached to his own power, his own identity as a kind of super-hero, Samson acts as if he is invincible. In the end, he tells Delilah the truth, that once his hair is cut he will become like any other man. As Samson is asleep in her lap, his hair is shorn and his strength leaves him. A band of Philistines binds him with "fetters of brass" (16:21) just to be sure. They also blind him.

Samson's attachment both to a person (Delilah) and to a thing (his elite Nazirite status) make him oblivious to the danger of his situation. His inability to know where he really stands—his disorientation—leads to his undoing. Because he can't imagine a world without his lover or a life without his position, he falls into a fatal trap that could probably have been sidestepped. After some time (enough for the text to tell us that his hair has started to grow back), Samson is dragged out of prison and brought into the Philistines' public arena so they can "make sport" (16:25) with him. It is at this moment, when the blind and groping Samson is being taunted, humiliated, and abused, that he expresses a death wish: "O Lord God, remember me, I pray to You, and strengthen me, I pray, just this once. . . . Let me die with the Philistines." (16:28, 30) Betrayed by the woman he loves, no longer the person he has been—or has seen himself as—since the moment of birth, Samson's self-destructive impulses aren't impossible to understand. He leans on the central columns of the arena until the entire structure collapses, killing everyone, himself included. If there is meaning in the event, if from the biblical perspective Samson's disintegration has led to some sort of a rebalancing, it is that the Israelite hero has had his final vengeance.

Our connections to individuals or things can be extreme, and they frequently lead to serious problems. For some, it is possible to reorient ourselves, and even become stronger, after having first gotten lost. But some attachments are so troubling that it is hard to find redemption in them. Perhaps the most common and ancient of these types is the attachment to *self*. In our era, we call it narcissism. In the biblical period, it was known as idolatry. Look at the story of the Tower of Babel (Genesis, chapter 11).

The great flood is over, the world has been reborn, and the people of the earth all speak in a single, universal language. They decide to construct a monument to themselves: "Come, let us build us a city, and a tower, with its top in heaven, and let us make us a name." (11:4) It is this primeval act of self-deification, of attention to and absorption with our own egos, that leads to a *de*tachment from God. How can we serve a Creator when we are overwhelmingly concerned with ourselves? In their pursuit of glory and fame (you can almost hear Kohelet muttering, "Vanity of vanities . . ."), the people of the world lose their way. As a result of their idolatrous behavior, their abandonment of God, they receive divine punishment. God scatters the people across the face of the earth and "confounds" their uniform language, splitting it into a multiplicity of different tongues. Now they are unable to communicate with one another. The tower is left standing, unfinished, a testimony to the spiritual and, ultimately, social fragmentation that they themselves brought about.

———

ONE WAY OF AVOIDING THIS CONDITION is never to get attached to any person nor any thing. As the great poet Rainer Maria Rilke writes, "Be ahead of all parting, as though it already were / behind you, like the winter that has just gone by." For him, as for many others, all encounters, all experiences, all of human life, is fragile and impermanent. The way we stay rooted in the present, the way we keep from losing ourselves in the gravity of this awareness, is to simply let it all go—from the very outset, before we get too entangled in that which can give us only confusion and pain.

That is one response to the challenge of the human condition, but it is a difficult one. Yet unless we want to disconnect fundamentally from the people and the world around us, we have to find ways of dealing with the experience of disorientation. As we have seen, there are many different catalysts for why and how human beings become lost. In most situations, however, it is also clear that the experience doesn't have to be a damaging one, that it can often lead to inner transformation and spiritual growth. The biblical prophets frequently speak of our need to be temporarily (but consistently) shaken free of our foundations, when they have disintegrated through complacency or moral corruption. The mystics advocate the scrambling of our souls as well. John of the Cross talks about the deconstructive aspects of the soul's "dark night" on its journey toward the divine light, while Rabbi Dov Baer of Mezeritch describes how the breaking down of our very sense of self—a brush with "nothingness"—is an essential stage in the path to God.

Human life is filled with twists and turns, struggles and challenges. It is perplexing, paradoxical, mysterious. The ways each of us choose to respond to that mystery, to the moments when we feel lost, determine the kinds of individuals we become and the legacies we leave to those who follow us.

TWO PANIC

Lent wings by my desire to visit the cinnamon shops, I turned into a street I knew and ran rather than walked, anxious not to lose my way. I passed three or four streets, but still there was no sign of the turning I wanted. What is more, the appearance of the street was different from what I had expected. Nor was there any sign of the shops. I was in a street of houses with no doors and of which the tightly shut windows were blind from reflected moonlight. On the other side of those houses—I thought—must run the street from which they were accessible. I was walking faster now, quite disturbed, beginning to give up the idea of visiting the cinnamon shops. All I wanted now was to get out of there quickly into some part of the city I knew better.

BRUNO SCHULZ, *The Street of Crocodiles*

IN ANCIENT GREEK RELIGION, Pan was a pastoral god of fertility, a merry, rather ugly man with the horns, ears, and legs of a goat. His job was to make flocks fertile, and though he was emotionally unpredictable and would occasionally frighten unwary travelers (sending them into a "panic"), he was associated with life and life-giving energy. It was only later that he began to take on darker, demonic shades, becoming less linked to vitality and growth than to alarm, horror, and hysteria. Being in the presence of Pan—something that had originally been thought of as a brush with fecundity itself—mutated into an experience not of transformation but of fear and loathing, one where confusion and the loss of confidence and stability overwhelmed, even crippled, the human soul.

We too can encounter Pan during our journeys, particularly when we become lost. One of the things that makes us feel this most acutely is having our job taken away from us. In many ways, what we do for a living most defines us and gives us stability. If that vocation is no longer a viable part of our lives, what we are frequently left with is the sensation that we have lost not just the rudder that guides us but the ship that keeps us from sinking. I know of many cases of people who have entered depressions, had marriages crumble, even committed suicide as a result of being let go from a company at which they had been employed for many years. Sometimes the person snaps and lashes out violently at his or her former employer or coworkers (think of the infamous examples of retribution killings by fired postal workers). In an era of wavering economies and sometimes dramatic downsizing by major corporations, this is a growing problem that is all too real.

Losing a long-held job can be a traumatic experience. Yet when our familiarity with and dependence on something become extreme—when they reach the level of addiction—its loss can be more traumatic. And that trauma, often manifested as profound panic, can take place even when it is possession of the object of our addiction that is itself the cause. There are many different kinds of addictions. We can get addicted to food, money, or sex, to other people (what popular culture calls "codependency"), to power, to drugs and alcohol. The proliferation and success of the many and varied AA-style groups around the country attest to the great problem with addiction in our society—as well as our society's great need to address it.

Danny was born into a large ultra-Orthodox Jewish family in Brooklyn. Like many of his peers, Danny was sent to study at a yeshiva, and by the time he entered adolescence he returned home to visit only intermittently. He was extremely close to his father, whom he looked up to as his most important role model. Danny knew his father was sick, but because he was not home on a daily basis, he didn't notice his father's deterioration. In fact, Danny interpreted his father's dividing his nights between sleeping in their home and at the hospital as a sign that he was getting better. The reality was that he had inoperable cancer and did not want his life to end in a hospital. Danny did not even know that his father was dying until one week before his death.

Danny was thirteen when his father died. For him (unlike the older members of his family), the death was sudden and shocking. Over the next several months, Danny turned his back on everyone around him. He was confused and angry. He had questioned God before while studying in yeshiva, but now he rejected God—something that was unheard of in his family and religious community. "I still believed that God existed," Danny, who today is twenty, tells me, "but I hated Him." As a way of trying to strike back at the Deity who had abandoned him, Danny created rituals of rage. "On the Sabbath," he says, "when using electric power is forbidden for Orthodox Jews, I would flick the light on and off in my room and say 'Fuck you' to God."

Eventually, Danny came to believe that God didn't exist at all, and that his religion and religious training were meaningless. He acted out against his teachers and rabbis, and at fifteen he was thrown out of his yeshiva. On the street and with no guidance from a father, Danny says he didn't know what to do with himself. Without a religious institution to rebel against, he began rebelling against secular society. Danny started deliberately breaking the law: He'd shoot out streetlights with BB guns and experiment with drugs and drinking. "The only thing I ever bowed down to then," he jokes, "was the god made out of porcelain."

Unable to exert any control over her son, Danny's mother

sent him to Israel, enrolling him in a work/study program in Jerusalem. There, alone, away from home, and looking to numb his pain, Danny began to hang out with a group of young, rebellious American Jews who had also been sent to live in Israel by concerned parents. Though he had smoked plenty of pot back in the States, his smoking became much heavier. At sixteen, Danny became a dealer—first of marijuana, then of acid, ecstasy, and harder drugs. He found a market for his dealing, and in time he was making good money and becoming known in Jerusalem's underground community as a go-to guy if you were looking to score something. He sold to the large circle of young American Jews studying or working in Israel, as well as to native-born Israelis.

Soon Danny started using the drugs he was selling. His earlier experimentation had grown into abuse, and in relatively short order Danny was sticking needles into his arms. He took some kind of drug every single day. His big highs were always followed by intense lows. As his addiction deepened, so did a depression. Danny stopped talking to people and isolated himself. He would spend days walking the streets of Jerusalem alone. He was arrested several times for drug possession. The police became familiar with him and began testing him intermittently for "dirty" urine. In the middle of all this, during those few brief moments he could climb out of the fog that seemed to envelop his waking hours, Danny understood he was a lost soul and in way over his head.

One night, in a period when he had given up hope of ever gaining control over his life again, Danny was about to take a cocktail of drugs made up of heroin, ecstasy, and various pills. It was a mixture and a quantity that would have probably killed him. Looking back on that night, Danny thinks it was an unconscious act of self-annihilation. But at three in the morning he telephoned a social worker who in recent months had been trying to reach out to him. Distraught and hysterical, Danny told her what he was about to do and pleaded for her help. As the social worker tried to calm him, he conveyed to her how terrified he was about his future, how he wasn't sure he would make it, and how if he did he would most likely end up either insane or, like some of his friends, in a morgue.

Danny's panic was brought on not because he was afraid of losing the drugs he was addicted to, but because the addiction had made him lose his life. Yet his panic had a useful and unexpected function: It forced him to visit a place he hadn't been in for many years—vulnerability. The phone call to the social worker was the first moment he had approached another person for help—or allowed another person to help him—in as long as he could remember. More than that, Danny genuinely *wanted* to be helped. By exposing himself to another human being, by showing her he had weaknesses and needed assistance, Danny chose interaction over inaction, relationship over isolation, life over death. That exposure turned out to be the tool that pried open his shuttered heart, the step he needed to take before he was able to get clean and return home.

———

THE BOOK OF FIRST SAMUEL offers a striking portrait of the role that panic plays in the life of one important biblical character. The prophet Samuel at first resists the people of Israel's call for a king. But after the turbulent and violent period of judges such as Samson, and in the face of persistent agitation among the masses for strong leadership against the Philistines, the aged Samuel (with God's reluctant consent) finally gives in. Under divine guidance, he selects Saul, a tall, handsome young man from the tribe of Benjamin, to be Israel's first king. Samuel puts a tremendous amount of pressure on the youth: "On whom is the hope of all Israel? Is it not on you, and on all of your father's house?" (9:20) The answer Saul gives him, which is reminiscent of the response of Moses to God's charge that he lead the Israelites out of Egypt, conveys his own reluctance to take on the role of redemptive leader: "Am I not a Benjaminite, from the smallest of the tribes of Israel and the humblest clan of all the tribe of Benjamin? Why have you then spoken to me like this?" (9:21)

Samuel, following through on his sacred duty, anoints Saul king, pouring a vial of oil over Saul's head and kissing him. He tells the young ruler that the spirit of God will soon enter him, that he will exhibit prophetic qualities and be transformed into another man. Though Saul has been charged with consolidating the weak and scattered forces of Israel into a powerful, unified army, he is a spiritual figure as much as a martial one. When Saul leaves the presence of Samuel, we learn that "God gave [Saul] another heart." (10:9) Then, as Saul encounters a band of prophets coming down a hill, he begins to prophesy with them—an external manifestation of the internal ecstasy that results from the king's receptivity to the supernal world.

In the first stages of his reign, Saul's authority and leadership are never questioned. As in the story of Samson, we see examples of his military exploits and acts of heroism against the Philistines. Yet Saul's confidence in his status, and eventually even his inner equilibrium, start to deteriorate. Out of impatience and concern that his army is deserting him, the king—going against Samuel's instructions—makes sacrificial offerings to God that the prophet was intended to make. Furious that Saul has violated his orders, Samuel condemns Saul's kingship, informing him that there will be no dynasty and that a new king will replace him. Later, during the battle of Michmash Pass, Saul decrees a fast for his soldiers for the duration of the fighting (ostensibly to win God's favor). While the Israelites eat nothing until the battle has been won, Jonathan, Saul's son, who had not been told of the fast, tastes some honeycomb that his troops chance upon in the field. When Saul discovers what has happened, rather than inquiring about Jonathan's errant behavior, the king immediately calls for his own son's death. But the soldiers, who had earlier covered up for Jonathan, intervene on his behalf and save his life.

After Saul's vilification by Samuel, the disobedience of his son, and the resistance from his soldiers, a growing sense of fear and paranoia begin to take over the king. All of this intensifies when God rejects Saul's kingship in chapter 15 and then commands Samuel to fill his horn with oil and go to Bethlehem in order to meet Jesse, from among whose sons God has chosen a new king. Afraid that Saul will kill him if he discovers his mission, Samuel enters the town under false pretenses and anoints David, the youngest of Jesse's sons, as the new Israelite king. David, unlike Saul, is not tall, which surprises the prophet. But God admonishes him: "Do not look upon his appearance or his stature. . . . For it is not as a man that God sees; a man looks into the face, but God looks into the heart." (16:7)

The spirit of God enters David—and leaves Saul, supplanted by an evil spirit that begins to haunt him. Saul is unaware that his kingship has just been usurped. Whether this "evil spirit" is a supernatural force, or an emerging, intuitive panic about his political and spiritual situation, is open to interpretation. But Saul orders his servants to find him someone who can play the lyre, in the hope that music will help to soothe his tortured soul. In a scene of intense irony, David turns out to be the musician Saul's attendants usher into the royal court. Not only does David's lyre-playing temporarily relieve the king's restive soul; Saul develops deep affection for him, making him his official weapon-bearer.

It is only after the charismatic David volunteers to do battle with and then defeats and beheads Goliath, the Philistine champion, that Saul starts to feel directly threatened by him. David's heroism on the battlefield, coupled with the troubled state of Saul's own psycho-spiritual health, leave the king feeling as if he is losing power and control. Saul starts to lash out, though at first discreetly. He offers his daughter Merab in marriage to David—but only if the young man will join the regular army. Saul strategizes: "My hand must not be upon him. Let the hand of the Philistines be upon him." (18:17) Saul wants David dead, but he wants someone else to get the blame. (It seems that David was a diligent student, since this is the same strategy he uses later to successfully eliminate Bathsheba's husband, Uriah, as we saw in the previous chapter.)

David declines the offer of marriage to Saul's daughter, but he does enlist with the Israelite troops. Rather than being killed by the Philistines, however, his prowess in battle makes him an even greater threat to Saul, to the extent that "Saul became David's constant enemy." (18:29) Saul is once more gripped by an "evil spirit." With David playing the lyre next to him, Saul, in an explosive fit of violence, tries to pin David against the wall with a spear. David evades him, leaving the spear stuck in the wall, and flees for his life. When Saul discovers that David has fled to the camps at Ramah and is hiding out with the prophet Samuel, the king tries, unsuccessfully, to have him arrested. When Saul then goes to Ramah himself, he is yet again overwhelmed by a spirit—this time the spirit of God. Unlike at the outset of his spiritual journey, Saul is now more a *victim* of prophetic inspiration than a beneficiary of it. He strips off his garments and prophesizes, lying naked "all that day and night." (19:24)

David leaves Samuel and is befriended by the king's son, Jonathan. The seemingly possessed Saul, now back in pursuit of his foe, learns that the fugitive he seeks has also been aided by Ahimelech and the other priests at Nob. If Ahab had his Moby-Dick, Israel's first king has his own "demon phantom" that takes over his life (and will lead to his doom). Saul, lost in his fears and suspicions, again lashes out, ordering not only the slaughter of the entire priesthood of Nob but also a massacre of the inhabitants of that sacred city itself. Saul then commits a further act of sacrilege. A major confrontation is about to erupt between the Israelite and Philistine armies. Saul calls on God for instructions, but the divine spirit, as well as his prophets and priests, have all left (or been killed by) him. In violation of his faith's clear prohibition against consorting with necromancers and mediums (it is a capital offense in the Bible), the desperate king turns to a "ghostwife" for guidance.

It is worth noting that it is Saul's heart (28:5), rather than his spirit, that propels him into this situation. With nothing to root down his soul, Saul's emotions overpower him. Do they spring from a heart of darkness (as 10:9 seems to suggest) or simply a human heart that has lost its capacity to control itself? Saul disguises himself and journeys to En-dor, where the sorceress calls up the ghost of Samuel (who has now died). "Why have you disturbed me by bringing me up?" asks Samuel. (28:15) Saul explains his distress to the prophet, who, instead of offering him assistance, denounces the king for his errant behavior. Samuel also informs Saul not only that Israel will fall to the Philistines, but that Saul and his sons will perish the very next day.

Saul has lost everything—his spiritual guidance, his authority as the ruler of Israel, even his sense of self. The desperation that grips him eventually drives him to fulfill Samuel's prophecy. The Philistines catch up with Saul and his troops at Mount Gilboa. They overtake and execute his three sons. Saul is wounded in his belly by enemy archers but survives. As he turned to his weapon-bearer David when his soul was afflicted, the king now turns to his new weapon-bearer for solace. He fears that the Philistines will defile him. "Draw your sword and run me through with it," Saul instructs his servant. (31:4) But the man will not obey him. Without a word, Saul takes the weapon from him and falls on it himself. Then, like the ending of a Shakespearean tragedy, his attendant takes his own life as well. The Philistines find Saul's body, strip off his armor, and nail his corpse to a wall.

Saul succumbs to his panic. His fears and anxieties lead him to terrible acts that we would not imagine a man in his position could ordinarily commit—attempted murder, the massacre of a community, sacrilege, suicide. He breaks the most fundamental rules in the Book. Yet from start to finish, there is an almost unimaginable amount of pressure placed on Saul—he is Israel's very first king, the chosen one whose sacred mission is to unify his people and singlehandedly save them from the mighty and brutal hand of the Philistines. Not surprisingly, Saul is reluctant to take on this messianic role. He is a human being, and like a human being his flaws, coupled with events and emotions that overwhelm him, draw him into a psychic labyrinth from which he never returns.

———

IT WAS KONRAD LORENZ, observing the behavior of animals, who perhaps most compellingly described the "fight or flight" response. When an animal is threatened (either by another animal or by a pack of them), it generally chooses one of two options: to fight for its life or flee for it. One of the most powerful photographs I have ever seen shows a baboon about to be killed by a cheetah. The picture, which I first saw as a child in a collection of photos from old *Life* magazine articles, is grainy and out of focus. But the terror in the baboon's face is crystal clear— as is the fact that it is going to lose the confrontation and its life. Unable to outrun the cheetah and with nowhere else to turn, the baboon, its mouth gaping in a Munch-like scream, faces the great cat. The baboon looks as if it is about to trip over its own legs and fall backward. The expression in its protruding eyes is one of desperation and defiance. For me, that baboon has always served as the epitome of the "fight" response, the last-ditch effort of a living being to lash out against its fate.

There are strong parallels in human beings. When we feel cornered, and when all seems lost, we sometimes panic and lash out at the wrong targets, or when we shouldn't attack at all. This is what happens with Saul, who strikes with fear and violence at those who are closest to him—his son, Jonathan, his servant, David, his priesthood, and ultimately even himself. What distinguishes humans from other animals is our ability to respond to trouble in other, less primal (and potentially destructive) ways. We can engage in dialogue and diplomacy, negotiate terms, and sometimes come to a compromise. We can also exercise patience. And we can experience hope.

The second response to danger that is common in animals and shared by humans is flight. While animals flee from a predator or a competitor out of the genetic instinct for self-preservation, human beings sometimes try to run away when we *ourselves* have become our own worst enemies. For that, we need a degree of self-awareness (not just of our physical but of our moral and spiritual selves) that seems improbable in the rest of the animal kingdom. In one of the Bible's very first descriptions of human beings, for instance, we see the paradigmatic example of such a phenomenon through the actions of Adam and Eve.

At the beginning of the third chapter of Genesis, God has just given Adam his partner and wife, Eve. They live in the Garden of Eden, and they are both naked. Neither feels shame. In a sense, both of them are like automatons, without any substantial self-consciousness, doing exactly what God tells them to do. Until, as we all know, the serpent comes along. It is only after the man and woman, at the coaxing of the serpent, eat from the Tree of the Knowledge of Good and Evil (which God has forbidden them to do) that an awareness of a nonmaterial dimension of themselves manifests itself. As the Torah states, "The eyes of both of them were opened, and they knew that they were naked; and they sewed fig leaves together, and made themselves loincloths." (3:7)

Adam and Eve hear God walking in the Garden. At this point God says nothing, yet the man and the woman hide among the trees—clearly showing that even without God's admonishment they realize that they have done something very wrong. Actually, after eating the forbidden fruit, they recognize that they have made two mistakes. The first was exposing their private parts to each other, an error that they quickly and calmly remedy. It is the second error, that of disregarding God's will, that is the real sin, and that leads to a far more panicked and animal-like reaction in them. Their "flight" response is no doubt rooted in a fear of punishment, but it is also linked to an awareness, and a uniquely human acceptance, that what they have done is wrong.

When God asks the couple, "What is this you have done?"

(3:13), it is one of the most pregnant questions in the history of the world. What Adam and Eve have done is lose innocence, lose immortality, lose the trust of their Creator. Yet what they have gained is a capacity for free choice and a more evolved sense of their identities that sets them apart from other creatures. Still, before the man and the woman go a step further (or backward) and eat from the fruit of the Tree of Life—thereby losing their very souls through a blatant act of self-deification—God expels them from the Garden to till the soil from which they were originally taken.

The flight impulse can drive a person to make damaging choices. Starting with Saul, and then continuing and expanding under the reigns of David and Solomon, the various tribes of Israel are all unified in a single kingdom. After Solomon's death, Rehoboam, his son and the crown prince, appears to have been accepted as the new monarch immediately and without opposition by the southern tribes of Judah and Benjamin. Yet in the north there is strong political ferment among the tribes, and Rehoboam needs their approval before he can rule effectively over the entire country. Representatives of each of the tribes of Israel are summoned to Shechem for Rehoboam's coronation (since Shechem, unlike Jerusalem, lay not in the south but in the heart of the territory of the northern tribes, the selection of this site may itself have been a concession on the part of the new king).

Rehoboam listens to the grievances of the dissidents from the north. Their leader, Jeroboam, presents the terms under which they will accept Rehoboam as king. Yet Rehoboam, against the counsel of his calmer and more experienced advisors, refuses to agree to any of their (not unreasonable) demands. In fact, he threatens to increase their burdens. Led by Jeroboam, open revolt erupts among the northern tribes. Fearing for his life, Rehoboam hastily calls for his chariot and flees to Jerusalem. The rebellious tribes declare their secession from the house of David and proclaim their own king, Jeroboam. After only a century of unity, the kingdom is divided. Rehoboam rules the kingdom of Judah, made up of just two tribes, while his rival Jeroboam leads the kingdom of Israel, composed of the ten tribes in the north. Initially, heeding the advice of the prophet Shemaiah, Rehoboam resists going to war against his northern neighbors. Later, out of desperation or the desire for retribution, he engages in bloody warfare with Jeroboam. As a direct consequence of Rehoboam's panicked reaction to the challenge to his leadership and running away from dealing with it in better ways, the kingdoms of Judah and Israel are torn apart and hostile with each another for hundreds of years, setting the stage for the violent and tragic conquest of a weakened land by the Babylonians in 586 B.C.E.

When we flee from difficult situations, we can end up in deep trouble. But we can also find ourselves in new, more positive places than we could have ever imagined. Moses, for instance, begins his career as the future redeemer of the enslaved Israelites by killing one of the Egyptian taskmasters, then fleeing for his life into the desert land of Midian. While his initial action is motivated by a sense of dread, it ultimately leads to a marriage, a position as shepherd of his father-in-law's flock, and an encounter with God (and a burning bush) on Mount Horeb. Or take the case of the prophet Jonah, who at first runs away from his divine mission—only to undergo a spiritual transformation in the stomach of a colossal sea monster. Or Elijah, who flees in desperation into the wilderness, where he too discovers his God, as well as the courage to fulfill his destiny.

We just don't know where our journeys will take us, even when we are in a state of panic. And at times our fight and flight reactions can seem indistinguishable from one another. Through his suicide, the figure of Saul embodies both responses: He strikes out at, while simultaneously fleeing from, life itself. What is the message we should take from all of this? That our motivations, as well as our final destinations, are ambiguous. Yet it is from the heart of ambiguity—the murky, sometimes scary terrain in which Pan would leap out at unsuspecting wayfarers—that new growth can emerge.

Human beings can panic under pressure. When that occurs, as we have seen, we regress to the most primal part of ourselves. That instinctive reaction can express itself through a violent eruption or a desperate escape. It can also lead to an extreme narrowing of our focus, making us incapable of seeing or dealing with anything other than the immediate situation. And if the panic is powerful enough, it may obliterate our ability to think. That is one of the reasons why pilots crash their planes and policemen shoot innocent people. When I was a college student in Jerusalem, I traveled during one of my breaks to the resort city of Eilat, on the shores of the Red Sea, to take a scuba-diving course. One of the requirements for certification was an under-water exam. At one point in the exam, I had to remove the regulator (which supplied me with air) from my mouth and, sharing my scuba partner's regulator, breathe with him from a single device. When one diver placed the regulator into the other's mouth, he was cut off from the air supply, functioning on what-ever remnant of air was left in his lungs.

As the air dwindled, and the intervals between each breath seemed to grow longer, I became agitated. Though I was sur-rounded by beautiful coral formations and stunning schools of fish, all I could concentrate on was that regulator. Our Israeli instructor, who was floating directly in front of us, seemed to melt into the seascape. There was nothing in the world but my lungs and the air and the ocean around me. Suddenly I swallowed some water. As I instinctively gasped for air, I swallowed more water. I couldn't breathe. An overpowering sense of fear gripped me. I was pure emotion, unable to reason. In this kind of situation, the worst thing you can do is grab your partner's regulator—it can damage the device and potentially kill both divers. But that's what I did. Luckily, as I started breathing again from his regulator, I calmed down, and we resumed the drill. And even though I ultimately passed my certification exam, I also received a reprimand from the dive master and a stern lecture on underwater protocol.

Some of the events in our daily lives can have a similar effect on us. When we lose that which had previously given us a feeling of stability and confidence (such as a professional position or a personal relationship), we can experience that same sense of fear, insecurity, and constricted focus. Yet a temporary and radical narrowing of our point of concentration may grant us certain benefits. It forces us to decide what is most essential to us, as well as what is expendable. It compels us to prioritize our lives and evaluate our goals. Frequently, it shows us—in an irresistibly elemental way—that, in the end, those very things we had earlier held in such high regard are in fact far less important than life and limb. Abraham Maslow wrote about a hierarchy of needs. But there is also a hierarchy of values. That scale is unique for every person. For it to become visible to us, however, and for us to then *act* on it in ways that can transform our inner and outer lives, we often need to have our complacency shattered by some external stimulus or circumstance.

Sometimes that external experience can paralyze us. In my work as a chaplain to federal law-enforcement agents, I have heard many war stories. But one of the most difficult things I've had to bear witness to was the grieving of a retired Secret Service agent, now in his late seventies, after the death of his wife. Roger had been married to her for over fifty years, and the majority of his life had been spent with her in it. Their marriage had been a very happy one—she had supported him through challenging times and had celebrated with him during festive ones. With her gone, Roger didn't know where to turn or how to live. "I feel paralyzed," he told me following the graveside service, seeming to choke on his tears. "I'm scared. I'm so alone. I don't know what to do." Through the support of his friends, the law-enforcement community, and counseling (as well as with the passage of time), Roger has been able to confront and cope with his loneliness and grief, and to gradually emerge from the forces that had threatened to immobilize him.

Roger made no rash decisions. Yet others, when in a panic situation, do. I know of many people who, after the death of or divorce from a spouse, remarry immediately. And countless single men and women of my generation, after they break up with a girlfriend or boyfriend, go from dating partner to dating partner, one after the other. Human beings behave in this way because most of us are afraid of being alone, and when we get involved in a new relationship too quickly it frequently turns out to be a mistake—sometimes resulting in even more pain than the initial breakup. Rather than sitting with and learning from our grief, we panic and jump into something we hope will numb us to it. This kind of unhealthy pattern is paralysis of a different order. For we move on in our lives, not because we have worked through our difficulties but because we are enslaved by them.

———

MARTHA IS A LAWYER who lives in Wisconsin. She has a strong, healthy marriage and a rich religious life. Several years ago, however, Martha felt as if everything in her world had collapsed. She had gone to her physician about a pain in her upper arm, and after the exam he suggested that she have a biopsy done to check for breast cancer (it had been quite some time since she'd had a mammogram). Breast cancer was something to which Martha had given a great deal of thought. Two of her friends had died from it—one at the age of forty-two and the other at thirty-eight. But the week after her exam, as she drove with her husband to the doctor's office to learn the results of the biopsy, Martha wasn't particularly worried. "I figured the odds were in my favor," she says today. "I had long counted on my friends' illnesses as my safety. I did the math. The chances seemed slim that I, too, would develop the disease."

Martha was sitting on the exam table when the physician entered the room. "It's a good thing we did the biopsy," the young man said matter-of-factly, "because we found a little cancer in there." Martha's mouth hung open. *A little cancer? Is this some kind of sick joke?* Her doctor went on to say that she would have to have more surgery, since the biopsy didn't remove the entire tumor. "He also said something about survival statistics," Martha recollects, "but I didn't pay attention. I don't remember anything else he might have said. My brain and my emotions were completely shut off. All I had at that instant were *physical* sensations. I felt like I'd stopped breathing. I couldn't move my body. My focus narrowed. I couldn't look straight ahead, or even look at my husband. It was as if I'd become a kind of automaton, just a suit of flesh on a rack of bones."

Martha was thirty-seven and had been married to her husband for four years. Yet in a single moment, as a result of a short rush of words, her entire world imploded. "Everything shifted and turned upside down," Martha says. "I was in a state of panic. I didn't know anything, and nothing meant anything. My universe contracted to a solitary point, a single fact: I was going to die. I was also going to die young. And I was going to die in pain. Everyone I knew died from the disease. No one survived. My life was over, right there, right then, in that doctor's office, and I couldn't even reach out to hold, or be held by, my husband. I was alone, stunned, dumb, my thoughts incomprehensible."

In the car on their way home, Martha's husband turned to her and said, "I want you to know that I won't leave you." The thought that he would abandon her at her time of greatest need hadn't entered Martha's mind; she had seen how much he had tended to one of their cancer-stricken friends in her final months, spending long hours with her in the hospital in the last weeks of her life. She died in his arms. Martha had no reason to expect anything less from him. But then the gravity of the situation hit her, and she had a sudden insight into her husband's seemingly cryptic statement: *He's been through this before. It ends badly. I'm going to do it to him again. I'm going to hurt him, cause him anguish and pain, and leave him alone. I don't want to do this, but that's how it's going to be.* She was filled with guilt and shame for subjecting her beloved husband to this traumatic experience that she was powerless to stop. "My mind scrambled to find ways to go back in time," Martha says, "to reel those words back into the doctor's mouth. Panic rose in me, drowning me, cutting me away from everything I held dear, setting me adrift. The sense of unreality was palpable, and somewhere in my mind I kept searching for a breach in order to tear this nightmare away and step into reality again. I wanted to die right then and there, as it seemed I was destined to hurt the most sacred person in my life."

Martha doesn't remember much from that first night after hearing the news that she had breast cancer. She thinks that they went out for Thai food with her mother (who had been informed of the disease by Martha's husband—she herself was not capable of giving her mother, who'd lost her own husband only three years before, such devastating information). "Everyone around me tried to pretend that everything was normal," Martha recalls. "It offended me. The earth beneath my feet had trembled, twisted, buckled. The world had opened up and, gaping, sucked my life into an abyss. Why would we want to talk about the food? All pleasure was gone. All hopes and dreams fled. I forced myself to eat, to interact. And as soon as we returned home, I went to bed."

It was in sleep that Martha found her only refuge from her panic and fear. For three straight days, she stayed in bed for four-teen hours or more; every waking hour was torture for her. She ached for her husband desperately, and that aching hindered her ability to reach out for him. He, on the other hand, touched Martha frequently, held her firmly in his arms, looked long into her eyes. "He was trying to figure out how to behave," she says, "how to serve me, how to help. His attention and love only cut into my heart more deeply. I felt disgust for giving him this burden, and I was powerless to lift it."

Martha was useless at her job. She spent hours sitting at her desk trying to come up with ways of escaping from the unreality of her experience. Finally she began to write notes to each member of the prayer group she belonged to. *I have just been diagnosed with breast cancer,* she wrote. *Please pray for me.* "I sent out fifty notes, each with that simple request. I didn't know what praying would mean for these people—I didn't know anymore what it meant for me. But in my panic, I could do nothing more for myself, so I could no longer afford the luxury of independence. I needed to rely on others; I needed to lean on them for a while. I had no idea how to imagine such a thing. I'd always been self-reliant. Still, I wrote my letters and sent them out into the world."

Slowly it dawned on Martha that she needed direct help. She had already taken the first steps by sending the notes to her prayer circle, but her terror and inability to truly function again hadn't subsided. She called one of the members of the group, a compassionate listener and someone Martha trusted, and tried to explain her many feelings and impulses. And then her friend gave her something she hadn't had in what seemed like forever: hope. "This isn't it, Martha," she said. "This isn't how it's going to end." In the days preceding the telephone call, Martha had never entertained the notion that she would survive her illness. In her mind, there was only one possible outcome. It wasn't the certainty of her friend's words, but the possibility that they might be true, that brought about a shift in her mind-set. "Suddenly there was a flicker of light," Martha says, "a glimmer of hope. Through the course of a long conversation, we discussed the different things I could do, in addition to surgery, to help myself, to heal, to be healthy. When I hung up the phone, I cried. Then I cradled my breasts in my hands and thanked the Creator for even the *possibility* of another chance."

Over the two weeks that followed, Martha concentrated on eating better, reducing stress, meditating—the things in her life that she could control. She is convinced that it was those actions, or even action itself, that kept her feelings of panic and helplessness at bay. Then she went in for surgery (a lumpectomy and lymph-node dissection). After a few days, the young doctor— clearly more comfortable with and adept at delivering good news than bad—informed Martha of the results. They had found no more breast cancer, and the lymph nodes had tested negative for the disease. Though Martha still held on to some of her earlier doubts and fears, she decided to trust in the process, in her spirit, in the ultimate good of Creation.

Martha began to move on with her life. But the traumatic

experience she had just been through had changed her. "For the first time in my life," she says now, "I was acutely aware that I had no guarantees. I'd grown intensely focused on the exhilaration, and yet also on the endless pain, of my new knowledge about being fundamentally alone in the universe. No one but me could live my life, and no one else could accompany me into my death." For Martha, this consciousness was liberating. Regardless of circumstance or suffering, she would strive to be healthy and positive in body, mind, and spirit. And she would not give up on hope, even when all seemed lost.

"I gained great clarity in my choices," says Martha. "After I worked through the panic and pain of the experience, everything became very simple. Separating what was important from what wasn't turned out to be easy. And I learned that I couldn't walk my old path again. I would no longer tolerate the things I'd put up with earlier—unreliable friends, stress, negativity. But giving myself over to others was perhaps the bravest and smartest thing I did then. The safety net of prayer beneath me was tangible, and it still is. Yet it remains the hardest thing—to ask others for their help." During the times in Martha's life she has felt lost since she was diagnosed with breast cancer (almost ten years have passed), she remembers and retrieves these lessons, and they help pull her out of the void. And though, as she says, Martha alone must live her life, her solitude is now surrounded by community: "Without the reflection from others, without the echoes of my ancestors' heartbeats, without the acceptance of love, I am nothing."

———

PANIC IS ONE OF THE MOST ALARMING and uncomfortable of the various stages we can go through when we feel lost. If and when it occurs, it usually takes place early on in our struggle, at a time when we are starting to recognize the depth and scope of our confusion. Panic can scare the hell out of us. It can force us to revert to our animal impulses, make poor decisions, experience profound insecurity, freeze up in a state of inaction. But it can also offer certain benefits, such as narrowing our point of concentration and helping us focus on what is really important to us, or driving us into unfamiliar terrain we would have otherwise been unaware of or avoided at all costs. It is in these new places that growth and transformation often become possible. While plunging us into a world of ambiguity and pain, panic teaches us that as human beings we have no alternative but to live (either in tension or in harmony) with them. The seeds of this wisdom lie in the soil of agitation, but it is a wisdom we ignore at our peril.

THREE LONELINESS

Alone, alone, all, all alone,
*   Alone on a wide wide sea!*
And never a saint took pity on
*   My soul in agony.*

SAMUEL TAYLOR COLERIDGE,
"The Rime of the Ancient Mariner"

AFTER THE INTENSE EXPERIENCES OF DISORIENTATION and panic, there may arise a period of calm, an eye in our existential storm. When we stand in this vacuum, it can feel very lonely. Trauma, as we have seen, frequently leads to transformation of some kind, but while we are in the vortex of what seems like a black hole, it is hard to be aware of anything other than our own solitude and pain. The Torah is filled with traumatic episodes, and one of the most disturbing is Abraham's attempted sacrifice of his son Isaac in the book of Genesis (chapter 22).

Much has been made of the verse in which we see Isaac next: "And Isaac went out to meditate in the field at twilight." (24:63) The classic rabbinical interpretation of this scene is that Isaac is performing his afternoon prayers. But the Hebrew word from which "to meditate" is derived *(la-suach)* has other meanings. It can also be interpreted as "to converse." Is Isaac really praying, or is he talking to himself? Is he quietly reflecting on life, or has he gone mad? Some modern commentators have argued that, in light of his near-slaughter at the hand of his father, Isaac is experiencing post-traumatic stress disorder. Whatever is happening inside Isaac's soul, he is alone—either out of choice or as a result of forces beyond his control.

It is not clear from the verse that Isaac's solitude involves pain. For it is only when the two are united that being alone turns into loneliness. What is clear is that the future patriarch has temporarily removed himself from his family and community, perhaps merely to mark a transition point in his life, perhaps to help him work through the psychological effects of a difficult, even damaging event. That same isolation is evident in the life of Moses. More than any other figure in the entire Torah (with the possible exception of Abraham), Moses is of absolute import to the unfolding destiny of the people of Israel. It is Moses who transmits God's ultimatum to Pharaoh, Moses who directs the Israelites through the desert, Moses who brings his community to the cusp of the Promised Land.

At several of the most important moments in his own life, Moses is alone. After he kills an Egyptian taskmaster and flees to the land of Midian, Moses, as we noted in the previous chapter, becomes a shepherd for Jethro, his father-in-law. One day Moses leads the flock "far away into the desert." (Exodus 3:1) It is there, by himself on Mount Horeb, that Moses encounters the voice of God in a burning bush. He is told that he will be God's messenger, the human conduit through which God will redeem the Israelites from their bondage. Moses initially resists the call. Part of his hesitation is certainly fear of confronting the Egyptian god-king. Part of it is also humility, as when Moses says to God, "Who am I, that I should go to Pharaoh, and that I should bring the children of Israel out of Egypt?" (3:11) But perhaps a hidden component of his resistance to the divine charge is a sense that his role as prophetic leader will ultimately separate—and at times alienate—him from his people.

Following the departure of the Israelites from Egypt, Moses guides them as they trek through the wilderness of Sinai. It is in this desolate environment that Moses again meets God. Three months after his people's release from slavery, Moses ascends Mount Sinai alone. There God tells him what he is to say to the assembled tribes so they can prepare for the great theophany, God's communication—using Moses as a mediator—of the eternal covenant with Israel. God appears on the mountain amidst thunder and lightning, but it is Moses who conveys God's words and will. After the revelation at Sinai is over, God tells Moses to ascend the mountain once more, by himself, to receive the stone tablets on which the commandments are inscribed. Moses places Aaron in charge of the community, then goes up to the mountain for "forty days and forty nights." (24:18)

Whether this figure is literal or not, Moses spends a significant amount of time in seclusion, isolated and often in communion with God. His long periods of separation from his people contribute to challenges to his leadership as well as to open rebellion; Moses is viewed by many of the Israelites with suspicion, resentment, and contempt. It is ambiguous as to how this affects the inner life of Moses. Does he accept his solitude as a necessary feature of his leadership? Or is he pained by it, experiencing his special and solitary existence not as a divine gift but a diabolical curse? Is Moses *lonely*? The Torah doesn't tell us in clear terms. At the end of the book of Deuteronomy, the Israelites stand poised to enter the Promised Land. Moses is an old man on the verge of death. He offers his final blessings to his people, then ascends to the top of Mount Nebo, where Moses is granted a vision of the land he will never set foot on. He dies alone, his burial place unmarked and unknown.

RELIGIOUS MEN AND WOMEN have known for millennia about the powerful role that solitude can play in our inner development. Individuals of diverse faith traditions went on solitary retreats and pilgrimages; some, like the early Christian desert fathers, lived alone in barren cells; others, like the hasidic mystic Rabbi Nachman of Bratslav, developed their own ritualized practices of intense self-seclusion. Many of the great and revolutionary spiritual leaders, such as the Buddha and the Ba'al Shem Tov, first removed themselves from the world before returning to it to share what had been revealed to them. What links all of these figures is not theology or worldview but a common understanding that solitude can promote insight as well as healing and personal change.

The fact that isolation can be transformative and therapeutic is rarely mentioned in today's psychological textbooks. The expectation in our culture is that satisfying personal relationships will provide us with the grounding and happiness so many of us crave—and that if they don't, there has to be something problematic with those relationships. As the Jungian psychoanalyst Anthony Storr argues, this expectation is exaggerated and distorts the nature of the human condition. Although love, friendship, and community are an important part of what makes life worthwhile, they are not the only source of fulfillment. What occurs in human beings when we are by ourselves is as valuable as what happens in our interactions with others.

Our capacity to be alone is connected with becoming aware of our deepest feelings, needs, and impulses, to self-discovery and self-realization. It can disclose to us just how narcissistic we really are, or it can show us how little we are concerned with our own well-being. Solitude is a teacher. But it is also a healer. One of the most ancient and vital Jewish mourning rituals is that of sitting *shiva,* of partially separating the mourner (who is prohibited from working during the observance) from the rest of his or her community for a period of seven days following the burial of a loved one. This practice acknowledges that coping with loss—bereavement—is a challenging, painful, largely solitary process that may be hindered rather than helped by distractions. As time passes, the mourner, still hurting, often comes to see that the meaning of life is not exclusively linked to personal relationships, that the life of a person bereft of those relationships has meaning as well.

This isn't an easy truth to absorb. Mara, an antiques dealer, had a relationship with her mother that was intensely symbiotic. Mara's mother was a survivor of the Holocaust, a member of a generation that had experienced unspeakable suffering. Though she had managed to escape from Europe and make it to America, she had not been able to save her parents or three sisters. All of them were murdered by the Nazis. According to Mara, one of the key themes in the household her mother later created and nurtured was that of an almost radical responsibility to one's family—a focus that emerged at least partly out of her guilt for having failed to rescue her own family in the Old World. Mara was raised with the mind-set that failure to protect one's kin was unacceptable.

Needless to say, when Mara's father died she felt an overwhelming responsibility to console and be present for her grieving mother. Mara was going through a major turning point in her own life then (she was in her thirties), having grown deeply disillusioned with her job after nearly a decade of work with the company. She decided to move in and live with her mother. For two years Mara offered her mother comfort and attention, while her mother gave her the anchor she needed at a time when she was unsure as to what direction her life should take. The two of them became more and more dependent on each other for their emotional nourishment. But suddenly Mara's mother was diagnosed with terminal cancer. As her mother began a gradual and painful decline, Mara's sense of obligation for her mother's emotional well-being shifted to one of duty to keep her alive. Mara remained in a constant state of "red alert," as she puts it, throughout her mother's illness.

Mara quit her job in order to devote herself to caring full-time for her mother. True to her family's values, Mara wanted to *save* her. But no one around her was acting similarly. Nobody had made her mother the center of their lives as she had. They just accepted her inevitable death. Mara fell into a panic, enraged that others weren't panicking as well. "Our world was ending," she remembers, "and everyone else was walking around as if this was okay, accepting it, taking it in stride. I hated the doctors. I hated the nurses. I hated my siblings." The fact that her mother thought no one but Mara could truly protect her intensified Mara's burden and feelings of isolation. The knowledge that nobody would or could devote themselves to her mother the way she had made Mara feel more alone.

"The sole focus of my life," Mara says, "was keeping her alive and out of pain from hour to hour. I became so compulsive that I believed my way was the only way to help her. I was so connected to her that I felt her pain. My siblings would come to visit her, but then they'd go home and live their lives. I lived under her roof. She slept in the 'sick room,' and I slept on the couch. This went on for two years." Even without the admonitions of her siblings, Mara knew that she was losing some of the most vital years of her life. But she had become impossible to reason with or even be around. Rationality had taken a back seat to the call of radical responsibility. Mara resented her siblings for having failed in their family's sacred mission, her father for having died, her mother for being sick and putting her in this situation.

Mara's feeling of solitude only increased when the morphine her mother was taking began to produce paranoid delusions. Her mother accused Mara, the person she saw most often, of ignoring her, of not doing enough to help her, of hurting her, at times even of trying to kill her. "She would say things to me," Mara recalls, "like, 'Can't you do anything for me?' and, 'You're only making things worse!' It was as if the person who'd given me emotional support my whole life was now suddenly, disturbingly, turning on and away from me." Mara felt that, despite her best efforts and absolute commitment, she was being abandoned. She felt truly alone for the first time in her life.

All of the pressure, pain, and guilt contributed to making Mara feel as though she was failing at the very project she had sacrificed everything for. "There was no reward, no redemption," she says. "Being a caretaker to the extent that I was isolated me from everyone around us. My world consisted of our living room and my mother's hospital bed. The focus of my care transformed into the focus of my existence. It gave me a purpose and an immediacy that others didn't and couldn't share. This all made me feel very lonely, cut off from the outside. If you add to this the fact that as all of this was taking place I was also losing my mother, well, you can imagine what a trial it was."

Neither Mara nor her mother liked hospitals, which was one of the primary reasons why so much of the activity surrounding the decline of Mara's mother occurred within the confines of their small house—a house that eventually came to feel like a prison cell. On Yom Kippur, the Day of Atonement, after two years of Mara's caregiving and her mother's physical and mental deterioration, her mother had a stroke. As a consequence, she was no longer able to swallow her pain medication and started to suffer terribly, crying out in agony. Since the physicians hadn't told Mara that she could administer the medicine to her mother through alternative means, she had no choice but to move her mother to the hospital. Two weeks later, she died.

Mara didn't know how to live without her mother. Over the preceding two years, the bond they'd always had had grown more powerful. After her mother's death, Mara felt guilty and entered into a depression. "No one could have done more for her," she says, "and yet she died anyway." But as she began to grieve, and as the initial trauma of her mother's death receded somewhat, Mara remembered something that her brother had said to her months earlier, something that only now was actually starting to sink into her soul. As it became ever clearer that their mother would not be well again, that in fact her death was imminent, Mara's younger brother told her that she was being cruel, that at this point she was keeping her mother alive more for *herself* than for any other reason.

But that insight was just the first step in a long and difficult process of healing. It took Mara another two years before she realized that in the end she didn't fail; her mother's death was completely beyond her ability to control. "Life is a wild beast, and so is death," she declares. "I used to be a control freak, but after the experience I had, I learned that no one is in control, that thinking and acting as if we have a capacity to direct our destinies is an illusion." Mara had also always thought that medicine was an exact science, that doctors were healers. Her mother's death demonstrated to her that the reality was different—that doctors weren't able to control the disease, or even the pain. These existential truths struck Mara like a thunderbolt and allowed her to start relinquishing her desire to direct, confine, and tame life in the ways she'd attempted to up till then.

During those years after her mother's death, Mara says that she "floated" in a state of inactivity, pitying herself and filled with horrible regrets. She experienced a profound solitude unlike anything she'd ever known before: "I had no job, no family, no significant other. With my mother gone, I had to return to square one. But the enforced solitude taught me many things. Humility, for one. I started listening to my own inner voice rather than struggling in futility to control my environment the way I'd been taught to. I also learned that I was far stronger than I thought I was. I did move on. I began a new career. I found a new voice and constructed a new life on the ruins of the old one. Earlier, I'd let external things, like a profession or a role, define me. After that period of sitting quietly by myself, it became me, and me alone, who defined my true identity. The sources of who I am are now internal. I am me wherever I go."

The slow and circuitous road to self-actualization forced Mara to rely on resources she had never fully accessed or depended on before. "Letting go of control and falling into your own self involves an enormous amount of trust," she says. In the aftermath of this painful episode, Mara found herself with little choice but to trust that there was some kind of redemptive power in the universe. She came to believe not just in the existence of God (an intellectual affirmation she had held for many years) but to actually *trust* God, to open herself up to the possibility of divine aid. That was a leap of faith Mara had never previously made. And it allowed her to connect with other people in new and more intimate ways: "I became less concerned with perfection in others—I saw that everyone is as powerless and vulnerable as I am. I became kinder, less demanding, more forgiving. I learned compassion. The best you can expect in life, from yourself and from other human beings, is good intentions. What I embrace these days isn't solitude but solidarity."

————

GRAHAM GREENE WRITES that there is a "panic fear" that is an inextricable part of the human situation. Yet solitude helps us get beyond the panic; it repairs and renews our souls when they feel crushed by the weight of ordinary life. It also allows us to move past merely finding our innermost selves to also *expressing* them, as in the cases of the countless painters, writers, and composers who segregated themselves from others in studios and attics in order to produce their creative work. Sometimes that solitude is enforced. Both Goya and Beethoven became deaf during their artistic careers, but each one utilized his feelings of isolation— and sense of freedom from the outside world—by creating new visions and compositions that reached heights of imagination and experimentation unattained by other artists. Dostoevsky's experience of seclusion and servitude in a Siberian prison camp permanently influenced his view of human nature, making him believe that individual self-expression was an essential human need that did not mesh with the demands of the state.

Solitude can also help catalyze spiritual expression. In the winter of 1934, Admiral Richard Byrd journeyed to Antarctica to man an advanced weather base. He insisted on going there alone. His mission was not just to make meteorological observations but, as he writes in the book *Alone,* "to taste peace and quiet and solitude long enough to find out how good they really are." Modernity makes the serenity of being by ourselves very difficult to attain, and in Byrd's time, with all the celebrity and attention that his earlier expeditions had brought him, he found it nearly impossible. Byrd felt that "a crowding confusion" was taking over his life—he felt lost. Although his initial goal was escape and renewal, what Byrd experienced was mystical union. While taking his regular 4 P.M. walk one day, he records in his journal, "I paused to listen to the silence. . . . Harmony, that was it! That was what came out of the silence—a gentle rhythm, the strain of a perfect chord, the music of the spheres, perhaps. . . . In that instant I could feel no doubt of man's oneness with the universe."

On a different occasion, Byrd refers to feeling "more alive" than at any other time in his life. For him, solitude had brought with it communion with the divine and an affirmation of human existence. "It was a feeling that transcended reason," he writes, "that went to the heart of man's despair and found it groundless." The language that Byrd uses to describe his Antarctic experience is strikingly similar to that of the mystics when they describe their experiences of union with God. As William James writes in *The Varieties of Religious Experience,* "This overcoming of all the usual barriers between the individual and the Absolute is the great mystic achievement." For religious as well as secular adventurers, attachment to the sublime often takes precedence over attachment to other people. Among members of some circles (such as celibate monks or the "lone wolf" characters for which the polar regions are famous), it was believed that ultimate fulfillment came not from human relationships and institutions but from a transcendent source—God, for example, or nature.

The spiritual event triggered in large measure by solitude had a permanent effect on Byrd's perception of himself and the world. While he had the majesty of Antarctica to help precipitate the experience, events of this type can occur in isolation without any added external factor. These transcendent experiences are linked to certain features of the creative process: What had formerly been a blank canvas, a hunk of marble, or an unfathomable idea suddenly becomes a wave of stars swirling above a church, a seated figure deep in thought, a new way of understanding space and time. States that take us beyond ourselves, whether metaphysical or inspirational, start when we first get in touch with ourselves. And for that, we frequently need to be alone. James claims that mystical states (like extreme isolation) cannot be sustained for long—most, he writes, last for half an hour. Many artists hold similar views on the duration of their own inspiration when it is at its apex. The fact that solitude can transform our lives despite such brevity demonstrates how powerful a tool it can truly be.

Maslow calls such a moment a "peak experience." In his view, the ability to have these experiences is a sign of inner health, a trait of the self-actualizing human being. Maslow claims that "the creative person, in the inspirational phase of the creative furor, loses his past and his future and lives only in the moment. . . . This ability to become 'lost in the present' seems to be a sine qua non for creativeness of any kind." Following this argument, a dynamic, creative individual needs consistent periods of freedom from other people in order to develop his or her work, as well as his or her character. The danger is when we slide from self-actualization to self-absorption, from a healthy respect for solitude to an embrace of it that leaves no room for others in our lives.

———

YET SOLITUDE IS NOT ALWAYS A COMFORTABLE EXPERIENCE. And when it is conjoined with pain, it becomes something else: loneliness. Brian is a successful middle-aged sculptor with a wife and two sons. For him, making art is a solitary activity. Being alone is essential for "having a dialogue with yourself," for allowing ideas to incubate, for concretizing them in bronze or clay. Brian has always believed in God, and that God is the ultimate Creator.

When Brian creates, he taps into his divine self—and in turn he finds his real self. Since God is one, Brian imagines that God's existence is very lonely but necessary. Creating in isolation is Brian's version of *imitatio Dei,* imitating divine behavior. Yet there was a period earlier in his career when the solitude that had led Brian to fame and fortune turned into a black cloud that nearly swallowed him.

By his late thirties, Brian had achieved what most artists only dream about. He was the talk of the art community, his work was being shown in galleries all over the world, and he was making loads of money. Within a single year, however, several events took place that plunged him into a downward spiral: He got married, his first son was born, and he turned forty. Brian, who was used to working by himself seven days a week, sometimes for fifteen hours or more a day, suddenly felt that for the first time in his life he had to compromise on what he loved more than anything. He didn't know how to deal with his new demands and responsibilities. Just a few years before, Brian was living alone in a garret, eating oatmeal and peanut butter and jelly sandwiches, struggling to find an audience; now he had a house in the country and was surrounded by people who wanted his attention. They also wanted his work, and the pressure to produce, coupled with Brian's own competitiveness and ambition, was becoming more than he could bear.

When his mother died, it pushed him over the edge. Brian's art left him unfulfilled, and soon he could no longer work at all. For two years, he fell into a deep depression, a depression he didn't share with anyone. Although he had everything he ever wanted, he did all he could to sabotage it. He canceled shows by saying he was sick; he held off dealers with various explanations and excuses for why he had no new pieces to give them. During dinner parties at his country house, he felt as though he was holding in a great secret from everyone around him, which made him feel more and more isolated. And he said nothing about his depression to his wife, for fear, as he puts it, he would "scare the shit out of her." His marriage would have crumbled were it not for the fact that his wife would not let him destroy it.

Those two years were a time of enormous loneliness for Brian. "I might very well have killed myself were it not for my son," he says now. "Suicide is a selfish act that leaves a lot of victims behind." Though he refused any medication, Brian started psychoanalysis. The childhood memories he started to excavate were not pleasant ones. And he grew to realize that part of what was happening in his life—his sense of despair and isolation—related directly to his fear that he would create similar unhappy memories in his own family members. What better way to prevent such an eventuality, Brian surmises his subconscious was then telling him, than by wrecking his family at the very outset? An exchange with his father during this period confirmed Brian's worst fears about the kind of parent he might become. After a holiday meal, he took his father aside and told him that, despite all his professional successes, he was in a state of clinical depression and barely able to function. His father's response: "Everyone should have your problems."

Brian's mother was an atheist and, throughout her life, remained adamant in her belief that there was no God. Brian was with her when she died, and her defiant atheism was like a slap in his face. His own belief in God had been a source of comfort and inspiration to him, and he wished that his mother could have shared it in the end. It was faith that helped Brian with his art, and that helped him to get through his depression. "I prayed that it would end," he recollects. "I reached deep within myself to try to emerge from the belly of the beast." He also thought about his son, how he not only loved him but actually *liked* him. Then his second son was born.

His depression left him suddenly and startlingly, just the way it came. "One day it went away," according to Brian. "The cloud just lifted. I felt like I had somehow ridden out this terrible storm that had entered my life." His career was in shambles, but over time Brian regained his artistic powers. With the help of his wife, he also resurrected his relationships with his family. "The loneliness and pain taught me some important lessons," says Brian. "I know now that we're all vulnerable, that something like this can happen to anyone. The experience also taught me humility about myself and compassion for others." It is often only after we pass through life's darker trials firsthand that we truly understand and empathize with the suffering of those around us.

———————

WE HAVE ALREADY SEEN how the Torah frequently gives us little information about the interior lives of its figures. In the case of Isaac, his silence following his near-sacrifice by Abraham makes his inner state ambiguous. Is he traumatized and lonely, or simply ruminating alone in a field? With the example of Dinah, it is perhaps easier to infer meaning from her silence. In the book of Genesis, Dinah, the daughter of Jacob and Leah, is assaulted: "And when Shechem, the son of Hamor the Hivvite, a prince of the land, saw her, he took her, and lay with her, and defiled her." (34:2) After he has raped Dinah, Shechem falls in love with her. He asks his father to meet with Jacob to gain his permission to marry her. Jacob's sons, incensed by the rape of their sister, devise a plan without their father's knowledge: They tell Shechem and Hamor that Dinah can marry outside her tribe only if all of their men are circumcised, in accordance with the law of Israel. Shechem and Hamor agree to the terms, and three days after the mass circumcision, while the men of the city are weakened and in pain, Dinah's brothers attack them. Shechem, Hamor, and all of the other males in their community are slaughtered.

Throughout these events, Dinah has disappeared from the story. We don't see her, we don't hear her, we know absolutely nothing about what has happened to her or how she feels. Everything that takes place occurs *around* her—without her input, without her consent, maybe even without her knowledge. We learn in verse 26 of the chapter that she has already been living in Shechem's house, for her brothers "take" her from it during their rampage. Yet again, she is treated as a passive object, first as a trophy of Shechem's power, then as a testament to her brothers' vengeance. When the slaughter is over, Jacob is angry with his sons. He is concerned not with the morality of the honor killings or with what was done to his daughter, but with the fact that his small tribe will now be a pariah in the region. Dinah's silence speaks volumes. Though she may not have been physically alone in this episode, her psychic isolation and social segregation must have been intensely hurtful. She surely experiences the most acute kind of loneliness imaginable.

When Isaac wanders alone at dusk, there is no action surrounding him, nothing to make his silence stand out in stark relief to any kind of a backdrop. This makes the ambiguity of his internal state more noticeable. With Dinah, the opposite is true. She is in great pain. Not just from the rape but from the way she is treated by the men in her life. Unlike Isaac, Dinah does stand out in relief in this tragic tableau: The ground is the flurry of activity revolving around her, the figure her silence and absence. This is not a situation in which solitude gives birth to a beatific vision; it is instead a case of existential loneliness of the highest and most traumatic order.

Jeremiah is a biblical figure whose anguished loneliness is beyond doubt. Sections of the book that is named after him contain what are known as his "confessions," emotionally vivid and intensely personal material that has no real parallel in the Hebrew Bible's other books. In these self-revelatory outbursts, the prophet lays bare his soul, in all its solitary agony. Jeremiah is speaking in his own name; the "I" he refers to in these passages is not God, as in the other oracular sections, but himself. The book of Jeremiah is thus a very atypical and interesting biblical text, for it gives us the prophet's public pronouncements of gloom and doom alongside his private thoughts and feelings when that catastrophe came.

The opening chapter of the book makes it clear that Jeremiah has been predestined for the prophetic office since before he was born. Jeremiah, like Moses and Saul, at first resists his call to divine service: "Ah, Lord God! Behold, I cannot speak. I'm only a child." (1:6) But God tells Jeremiah not to be afraid or reluctant to embark on this journey, that God will be with him and aid him during the difficult times ahead. The prophet is warned of a coming disaster that will arise in the north. He does not yet know that that disaster will take concrete form in the Babylonian siege of Israel, but he does know that his sacred task as a prophet is to sound the alarm among his people and urge them to repent of their sins.

Jeremiah fulfills his mission. He warns the Israelites of the coming calamity, the invasion that God is orchestrating—using Babylonian soldiers as God's agents—as punishment for their moral and spiritual transgressions. But he also expresses the pain he is experiencing as the lone harbinger of such ruination. "O my bowels, my bowels!" Jeremiah cries, "I writhe! O chambers of my heart! My heart is a storm within me, I cannot be still. . . . Laid waste of a sudden my tents, in an instant my curtains.

How long must I see the standard, hear the blast of the horn?"
(4:19–21) Whether the prophet is describing a present event or
having a premonition of a future one has little bearing on the
inner torment his prophetic detachment causes him.

Jeremiah is nevertheless ambivalent about his people. He
grieves passionately for the Israelites: "Grief has overcome me,
my heart is sick. . . . For the hurt of the daughter of my people,
I am broken. I am thrown into gloom; dismay has seized me.
Is there no balm in Gilead?" (8:18, 21-22) But he also recoils
from them and their sins: "O that I had in the wilderness a way-
farer's lodge, so I could leave my people, and get away from
them! For they are all adulterers, a gang of criminals." (9:1) The
irony of Jeremiah's isolation is that he is lonely *precisely* because
he stands in the thick of his people—for him, solitude is far better than the company of a community like his. Yet the prophet
has no choice. God selected Jeremiah, set him apart from the
rest of his people, and with that choice sentenced him to a life of
loneliness: "You seduced me, God, and I let you; you seized me
and overcame me. I have become a daylong joke, they all make
fun of me. . . . Ah, the word of God has gotten for me scorn and
endless abuse." (20:7–8)

Although Jeremiah's relationship to his community is marked
by ambivalence, his relationship to his calling is rooted in open
conflict. Even when he tries to free himself of the burden of
prophecy, he is pulled back to it: "If I say, 'I will forget him! I will
no longer speak his name!' then it is in my heart like a burning
fire shut up in my bones; and I struggle to hold it in, but I cannot!" (20:9) Despite his desire to escape the derision that his
office has brought him, Jeremiah confesses that he is unable to
prevent himself from speaking the word of God. This is not surprising, since the book of Jeremiah begins with God reaching
forth, touching the prophet's mouth, and placing divine words

within it. Jeremiah has become a vessel for God's message, and he now fully understands the consequences. "Not for me to sit with the crowd," he says, "laughing and merry. Gripped by your hand I did sit all alone. . . . Why, O why, is my pain without end, my wound ever worse, defying all cure?" (15:17-18)

Jeremiah reaches the point of almost suicidal despair. His language is among the most poignant and anguished in the entire Bible: "Woe is me, my mother, that you bore me to accuse and indict the whole land! Neither lent I, nor loan received, yet all of them curse me." (15:10) For someone who has done nothing more than to be true to his vocation, Jeremiah has suffered far more than he deserves, and he later wishes he had never entered the world at all. "Cursed be the day," he says, "on which I was born! The day my mother bore me, let it never be blessed! Cursed be the man who brought the news to my father, 'You have a son!' . . . Because he killed me not in the womb, so that my mother might have been my grave. . . . Why did I come forth from the womb to see but trouble and grief, and end my days in shame?" (20:14–15, 17–18)

This is a man traumatized by his isolation. In the biblical context, his words border on blasphemy. Yet while Jeremiah probably never achieved inner peace, or even completely reconciled himself to his fate, he does come to understand that he has no alternative but to continue as the prophet he had been called to be in his youth. The confessions serve in part as his catharsis, solitary acts of self-expression and self-revelation that became ritualized in some of the later Jewish and Christian pietists and mystics. Jeremiah finds a vehicle for surviving the more painful aspects of his solitude, and in doing so provides a model of strength and perseverance for us all.

There are many things that happen to us during our lives that can leave us feeling confined and alone. Some of them we choose;

others find a way to choose us. But we can learn something from all of them, even the darkest and most extreme. There are accounts of how even solitary confinement imposed by enemies can sometimes catalyze valuable and transformative experiences. Arthur Koestler describes the solitude of his imprisonment in Spain, and how grateful he was that he did not have to share his cell with another inmate. He felt that his isolation helped him to appreciate and sympathize with his fellow prisoners. Koestler lived a solitary existence for some time, but he believed that that solitude connected him to a higher level of reality, transferring him from what he calls the "trivial" plane to the "absolute" one. He claims that solitude put him in touch with a "feeling of inner freedom, of being alone and confronted with ultimate realities instead of your bank statement. . . . Not in space but in spiritual space. . . . So you have got a dialogue with existence. A dialogue with life, a dialogue with death."

Wherever we are in our lives, we sometimes need that "spiritual space"—that radical solitude—to link us with ultimate reality, with what holds meaning and what doesn't, with who we are and who we want to be. In one of his poems, Delmore Schwartz refers to the human heart as "the lonely room where the self must be honest." Whether our solitude is voluntary or enforced, pleasant or painful, is less important than that it transports us to the seat of our souls, the place where we have to face ourselves *by* ourselves. No one can or should take on that all-important task for us. Call it spirit or heart, something we uncover or something we construct—but know that that place is the terrain of ultimate truth, and a region we must navigate through (or simply bear) if we are to continue in a grounded way on our journey.

FOUR YEARNING

He is much fish still and I saw that the hook was in the corner of his mouth and he has kept his mouth tight shut. The punishment of the hook is nothing. The punishment of hunger, and that he is against something that he does not comprehend, is everything.

ERNEST HEMINGWAY, *The Old Man and the Sea*

IT IS ONE THING TO GET IN TOUCH with our heart and soul. It is another to express what we find there honestly and openly. As we have seen in the case of Jeremiah, what the prophet expresses is pain, and his desire to be free of it—by any means necessary. We all have experiences that cause us hurt, that make us feel alone in the world. Yet once we move beyond our solitude and suffering, and if we dig deeply enough, we find that there is usually something else inside us, something that is hidden at times, waiting to be expressed. An inner hunger, a yearning for what we have left behind. Or for what we want but don't yet possess. Or even for what we already have and are afraid of losing.

The triggers for our feelings of yearning are complex, but often they involve being in a state that leaves us, at best, uncomfortable and dissatisfied, or, at worst, hurting. As an emotional phenomenon, yearning is more an expression of the heart than of the brain. It is not always rational, and it can frequently be rooted in memories or visions that are romanticized and utopian. In chapter 13 of the book of Exodus, for instance, the Israelites have just been led out of bondage and are now on their way to the Promised Land. They do not take the easier route along the Mediterranean coastline, however, because it is under the control of the powerful Philistines. Instead, God directs them to travel by way of the desert to the Reed Sea. Pinned against it by Egyptian horsemen and soldiers, whom Pharaoh, with vengeance on his mind, has ordered to pursue them, the newly freed Israelites become panicked. "Because there were no graves in Egypt," they cry out to Moses, "have you taken us away to die in the wilderness? . . . Did we not say to you in Egypt, 'Leave us alone, so that we may serve Egypt'? It would have been better to serve Egypt than to die in the wilderness." (14:11–12)

As a result of their desire to escape, the people of Israel are willing to choose the certainty of slavery over the promise of freedom. They, like many of us, long for the security of what they have already known and experienced more than the challenge of an unknown and as yet unrealized future. Even after God's parting of the Reed Sea and their rescue from the Egyptians, the Israelites, now facing the peril of starvation, confront their leaders: "And the whole congregation of the children of Israel murmured against Moses and Aaron in the wilderness: and the children of Israel said to them, 'We should have died by the hand of God in the land of Egypt, when we sat by the flesh pots, and when we ate our fill of bread; for you have brought us out into this wilderness to kill this whole assembly with hunger.'" (16:2–3) Their yearning to get out of their dilemma drives them to do three troubling things: First, it makes them look for someone to blame (they essentially accuse Moses and Aaron of murder); second, it compels them to sentimentalize, idealize, and distort their past; third, and most disturbing, it reveals a wish for death, the ultimate escape from their hardship.

Yearning can be dangerous. But a dissatisfaction with what is, and a craving for what might be, are fundamental aspects of being human. Samuel Johnson writes that the present passes so quickly that it is hard to think in any way other than in terms of the past or the future. Some thinkers on evolution have argued that humanity's extraordinary success as a species is rooted in its discontent, which drives us to use our imagination and inventiveness to survive and conquer. Still, we must be careful that our dissatisfaction and hunger do not drag us to the edge of a moral or psychological abyss.

———

WHEN OUR DESIRE AFFECTS US IN POSITIVE WAYS, it can help to pull us *out* of treacherous terrain. Cassandra is a successful entrepreneur with a husband and three children. Despite being one of the busiest people I know, she, along with her family, became one of the founding members of a new Jewish congregation in a major metropolitan area. You would think that this fact indicates a long-held and passionate embrace of Jewish life and identity. But it doesn't. Cassandra came to this point in her life circuitously, after years of soul-searching and a gnawing hunger to know who she really was—an awareness of her family history and religious roots that had been concealed from her.

As a child growing up in an affluent New York suburb with a heavy concentration of Jews, Cassandra celebrated Christmas every year. Her family belonged to a Unitarian church, and she remembers an occasional midnight mass or two when she was a very young girl. Hearing anti-Semitic comments from her parents was not uncommon. Cassandra's mother discouraged her from having Jewish friends. Not only had Cassandra never attended a bar or bat mitzvah in her predominantly Jewish community—she didn't even know what one was. Then there was the summer camp. Cassandra knew German because her parents spoke it at home (they were from Czechoslovakia); until she was eleven, she was sent each summer to a bleak town in northern Germany to attend a camp where German was the only language that was spoken. Many of the songs she sang there, Cassandra has since learned, were modified from original Nazi lyrics.

Cassandra's heart told her that something wasn't right in this picture. She felt an unusual preoccupation with, and a disingenuousness about, Jews and Jewishness. Whenever she tried to talk to anyone about it, Cassandra hit a brick wall, and the subject was quickly changed. Despite all appearances to the contrary, and although she didn't "know" she herself was Jewish, Cassandra somehow intuited that she might be. But she wasn't certain. As she grew older, she longed to learn the truth about her origins—and herself—more and more. In ninth grade, while she was living away from home at a New England boarding school, Cassandra's roommate looked at her incredulously one night as they were discussing the matter and declared, "With a last name like yours, of course you're Jewish!"

That's when it all started to click. Cassandra began to confront her parents directly, to communicate to them how much she wanted them to tell her the truth—a truth she already grasped. They always evaded her questions or said she was wrong. When Cassandra heard from an uncle that a great-grandfather had written an ethical will, and that he had been a leader of Prague's Jewish community and written in his will that his future progeny should honor their religious heritage, another relative denied the document's very existence. "You must be dreaming," he told the excited high school student. But the more she faced resistance and denial, the more resolute Cassandra felt in her belief about her Jewish identity. "It was unreal," she says today. "I encountered layer upon layer of deceit and lies. It was infuriating. I was so frustrated."

At boarding school Cassandra felt like the "token Jew." Yet by the time she got to college, she had grown more comfortable expressing her Jewishness to the outside world—though she was still ambivalent about it. One Rosh Hashanah, Cassandra went with her boyfriend to a synagogue for services. It was the first time she'd ever set foot in a Jewish house of worship. "I still remember the excitement and trepidation," she says now. The synagogue itself was grand and impressive, and she felt that the community members were welcoming. The experience— in essence a reconciliation with her past as well as a kind of reunion with her spiritual family—was transformative. "I felt surrounded by a rich heritage," says Cassandra, "and a real connection to a community of Jews from throughout the ages and from all around the world, all celebrating the same holiday of renewal and rebirth." Though she couldn't understand a word of the Hebrew liturgy, she didn't care. Cassandra was deeply moved and comforted by the rituals, and rejuvenated by the meaning of the holy day. Her soul felt fed for the first time she could remember.

Once she had become a young woman and begun building her life, more fragments of Cassandra's family history began to emerge. In 1991, she traveled to Prague with her family. It turned out that her parents were Jewish war refugees who had grown up in the Czech capital. They had come from very wealthy families, the upper echelon of the German-speaking Jewish social elite in Prague. The wealth and influence of their respective families helped them to escape from Europe before the Holocaust consumed their community. Cassandra's parents constructed a new life for themselves in the United States, one that didn't just hide but—through words and deeds—tried to obliterate their Jewish roots. (Ironically, despite the deep discomfort her father felt about his identity, he had saved many Jews during the war from certain death.) Her mother was tense the entire time in Prague; Cassandra herself was uncomfortable at first, until her father led her to the grave of the great-grandfather she'd only heard rumors about.

Cassandra resolved that if she had children she would never put them through what she'd experienced growing up—feeling lost. She wanted them to have strong and authentic foundations and to know exactly who they were. When Cassandra's father died, that desire for a spiritual anchor surfaced very powerfully. "There was no funeral, no ceremony, nothing," she told me. "It was as if he just evaporated." Whether her father would have wanted a ritual or not—and her mother clearly wanted nothing of the sort—Cassandra yearned for some formal observance to mark the closure of his life. She wanted something that felt right, and she would have settled for almost anything; what she really wanted, though, was something Jewish. But her hunger was yet again unsatisfied.

Cassandra fell in love with a Jewish man and had a beautiful Jewish wedding—two important events that, unlike her upbringing, were the result of her own choices and commitments. She is raising three children in the heritage of their ancestors, and she and her family are helping to create a vibrant new synagogue. "Starting something fresh and new is really attractive to me," she says. "I don't want to wallow in the past or romanticize it—I just want to move on into the future." For Cassandra, moving into the future *is* in a sense a confrontation with the past, and she is well aware of the symmetry. But sometimes she wonders: Is her embrace of her Jewish identity a consequence of her genuine desire for it, or instead a reaction to her parents' deceit? She admits that human motivations are complicated, and that she will probably never know for sure. "I'm just at the beginning of my journey back," she says. "Even though I get very emotional at services, and even though I want to dig deeper and know more about my tradition, I have ambivalent feelings and most likely always will. The powerful connections I feel today for what I've found are often matched by equally powerful feelings of sadness for what I've lost."

———

THERE IS A MAJOR DIFFERENCE between reconstructing or remembering the past and wanting to return to it. When the past is memorialized, it can help to ground us as we live our lives in the present. When we *worship* the past, it can paralyze us, prevent us from living in the moment and moving on to wherever it is that our lives are meant to take us. Following the destruction of the temple in Jerusalem in 586 B.C.E., thousands of Israelites were forcibly deported to Babylonia, where they began to develop new communities. Many of them reluctantly accepted their diaspora situation and conditions; they created new offices (such as the scribe) and new rituals (such as the public reading of the Torah) that fit better with the Babylonian context and culture. They had no choice if they wanted to maintain a religious way of life outside the land of Israel. Others viewed life in Babylonia purely as exile, yearning for a (recollected) past and desiring to restore spiritual life to the way (they imagined) it used to be. For these people, it was probably almost impossible to move on.

In Psalm 137, most likely composed during this time, we see a powerful expression of longing for the past and difficulty in continuing with the future: "By the rivers of Babylon, there we sat down, and O we wept, as we remembered Zion. We hung our lyres upon the willows in its midst. For there they who carried us away captive asked us for a song; they who ruined us asked us for celebration, saying, 'Sing us one of the songs of Zion!' How shall we sing God's song in a foreign land? If I forget you, Jerusalem, let my right hand forget its cunning. If I do not remember you, let my tongue cleave to the roof of my mouth." (137:1–6) This psalm is famous because of its beauty and poignancy. It reflects profound hunger on the part of its writer and the members of the community he or she speaks for. And it demonstrates how our tears must first dry before progression is possible, how the passage of time is vital in the evolution of a memory, transforming it from one that cripples us into one that anchors and inspires.

The authorship of the book of Lamentations is unclear. Because of the depth of its pathos, however, religious tradition attributes it to Jeremiah, the quintessential prophet of despair, a person who had witnessed the horrors of the Babylonian conquest and desecration of Jerusalem. Whoever wrote the book, it was someone in deep mourning over the loss of Israel's spiritual center. "How does the city sit solitary," the author laments, "that was full of people! How has she become like a widow! She who was great among the nations, and princess among the provinces— how has she become a vassal! . . . The ways of Zion do mourn, for none come to the sacred assembly; all her gates are empty; her priests sigh, her virgins are afflicted, and she is in bitterness." (1:1, 4) Unlike Psalm 137, the book of Lamentations goes on to place the blame for this desolate scene as much on the Israelites as the Babylonians; after all, as Jeremiah pointed out in his own book, it was their sinful nature that brought about the dire situation. What this author is expressing is an aching about the past without any sentimentality or nostalgia. He (or she) is well aware of what has been lost—but also aware of why.

The biblical book concludes with a plea (which also appears in the Jewish liturgy) that shows the author is very much living in the present yet still clearly attached to the past: "Turn us to you, O God, and we shall be turned; renew our days as in earlier times." (4:21) This is an individual—and a community—dealing with a spirituality of the here and now, but utilizing the past as a paradigm for how they as well as God should behave. The book's excessive emphasis on Israel's sins, and its inclination to blame the victims rather than the criminals for all of the death and destruction, is disturbing to many modern readers, myself included. But its remembrance of things past, coupled with a focus on the present, is healthy and brave, particularly for a people suffering the aftereffects of national trauma.

———

It is not always the past that we crave. Sometimes we yearn for the future, a state that is not old and familiar but new and pregnant with possibility. While both types of yearning share a dissatisfaction with life as it is and a desire to escape the burden of the present, each has a different way of distorting reality. The former perverts it through nostalgic recollections of the "good old days," which often fail to incorporate the more problematic dimensions of the way things really were. The latter twists reality by hungering for something that by definition does not yet exist, as well as by constructing idealized fantasies about what that nonexistent thing ought to be. Still, just as there are positive aspects to our longing for what once was, there are benefits to our imaginings of what might yet be.

The negative examples of these utopian visions are well documented in the political arena: the Soviet Union, communist North Korea, fascism, the Nazi regime. But they exist in the spiritual realm too, usually embodied in certain messianic movements. The messianic impulse, like most utopian impulses, is a binary one—it can lead to great beauty or stark horror. Many cult leaders have built communities around themselves and the idea that they were creating models of the perfected spiritual life. As diverse as some of these cults are, they frequently share utopian elements in their institutional frameworks, such as common ownership of property and income, mixed-race living conditions and marriages, tightly regimented (or "harmonious") behavior, and absolute submission to a leader, doctrine, or goal. It is not unusual for a cult leader to claim that he himself is the Messiah, personally anointed by God to save the world. In this context, the messianic often hides the malevolent. These spiritual utopias can exact a gruesome price: either the lives of the cult members through sacrificial—or, in cult language, liberating—acts (as in Jonestown and Heaven's Gate), or their and other lives through an apocalyptic war that the cultists work to bring about (as in the Branch Davidians and Aum Shinrikyo).

Christianity, Judaism, and Islam have had their own dark histories and versions of dangerous messianic movements, sometimes with catastrophic results. Thousands were slaughtered as the Crusades tried to purge the world of heathens who were holding back the kingdom of heaven. Families and communities were torn apart as Jewish men and women sold all their property and followed the false messiah, Shabbatai Tsvi, across the Mediterranean. Just last year, fanatical followers of Osama bin Laden, in an attempt to galvanize an international jihad against Western infidels, crashed airplanes into the World Trade Center and the Pentagon, murdering thousands of innocent people. These movements, and the leaders who create them, feed off the desperate longing that so many of us have for a future world we imagine to be perfect. Yet some messianic aspirations and visions, especially when they are protected from exploitation and perversion by normative religion, are not dangerous. Instead, they can direct and inspire us to improve—and eventually redeem—the world in which we *do* live.

The book of Isaiah contains one of the most widely known and beautiful visions of the messianic age. Early on in the text, as the prophet begins to paint his picture of the "last days," Isaiah describes them as being free of war. "They shall beat their swords into plowshares," he says, "and their spears into pruning hooks: Nation shall not lift up sword against nation, nor shall they study war any more." (2:4) He also describes them as being free of the uncertainty and ambiguity that plague us; the messianic era will be one of total clarity: "The people who walked in darkness have seen a great light; they who have dwelled in the land of the shadow of death, upon them has the light shone." (9:1) During the time of the Messiah, the world will be united and harmonious, liberated from violence, pain, ignorance, and injustice. "The wolf shall dwell with the lamb," Isaiah proclaims, "and the leopard shall lie down with the kid; and the calf and the young lion and the fatling together. . . . They shall not hurt nor destroy in all my holy mountain: for the earth shall be full of the knowledge of the Lord, as the waters cover the sea." (11:6, 9)

Isaiah's vision offers more than a portrait of the messianic era. It gives us clues as to what we need to do *now* in order to bring about that era. If we view his words and images as prescriptions for our own time, and not just projections about an age to come, we become aware of a new dimension to our lives.

When we listen to a voice from the past, bear witness to a vision of the future, and work to make both of them active realities in our present, then, in a mystical sense, we transcend time. We gain a taste of eternity here on earth. What are the things that Isaiah is urging us to do today through his depiction of the end of days? To eliminate war and violence by channeling our destructive energies in constructive ways. To usher in peace and harmony by unifying those who are opposed to one another. To act with spiritual wisdom, and to spread that wisdom throughout the world.

Yet how can a vision of a world that is so beyond us motivate us to devote our lives to working to achieve it? In the Renaissance literary convention known as courtly love poetry, a union with the object of the poet's passionate longing is never achieved, never consummated. The love object (a woman) is, according to this convention, described by the poet in exaggerated, idealized terms. She is more to him than a human being—she is a model of perfection, the embodiment of beauty, virtue, truth. The beloved woman becomes the source of meaning and inspiration to the poet; she grounds his life, gives it purpose, and draws him to her by her very presence. Though no marriage between the two occurs, the craving that connects the man to the object of his desire excites his heart and motivates his actions. A similar dynamic can take place between humanity as a whole and our lofty visions of the messianic era. Our intense yearning for an idealized, perhaps unreachable goal can inspire and motivate us, giving our lives purpose, meaning, and joy. We strive for the messianic objective because we (like the smitten poet) want to be *worthy* of it—and because little else ultimately matters.

Another memorable example of a vision of the messianic age appears in the book of Ezekiel. In chapter 37, God carries the prophet through the air and places him in the middle of an open valley filled with dry bones. God says to Ezekiel, "Prophesy over these bones, and say to them, O dry bones, hear the word of the Lord. Thus says the Lord God to these bones: 'Behold, I will cause breath to enter into you, and you shall live; and I will lay sinews upon you, and I will bring up flesh upon you, and cover you with skin, and put breath in you, and you shall live; and you shall know that I am the Lord.'" (37:4–6) Ezekiel follows God's command, and the myriad separated bones join together into full human skeletons, which are then encased with sinews and skin. Using Ezekiel again as an intermediary, God calls forth breath from the four winds, infusing the skeletons with it and giving them animation. They rise in unison, fully alive once more.

God explains to Ezekiel that the bones in this prophetic vision represent the members of the house of Israel, who have been complaining in their time of trouble that they feel like "dry bones," hopeless and cut off from divine aid. God instructs the prophet to speak to the Israelites in God's own words, saying: "Behold, O my people, I will open your graves, and cause you to come up out of your graves, and bring you into the land of Israel. . . . And I shall put my spirit in you, and you shall live, and I shall place you in your own land." (37:12, 14) In its historical context, Ezekiel (like Jeremiah) is prophesying to a people living in exile from their ancestral homeland, and he is addressing their yearning for redemption on two very different levels: First, on the "micro-messianic" one, he is assuring the people of Israel that they will one day return to their national home; second, on the "macro-messianic" level—the level of aspiration that is shared by most of humanity, regardless of religion or nationality—he is promising them that, even after they die, they will live again.

Most of us hope, and many of us believe, that our souls will live on in some way beyond this world, that we will participate in eternal life. But Ezekiel's vision of an afterlife takes specific form in bodily resurrection. (Isaiah's messianic vision involves the same promise, as when in verse 26:19 he says: "The dead of your people shall live, my dead body shall arise. Awake and sing, you who dwell in the dust.") Resurrection has always been a controversial theological topic, among Christians as well as Jews. In the context here, it represents a synthesis of a longing for the past as well as for the future. Eternal bodily life is part of the human makeup in the Garden of Eden—until Adam and Eve lose it through their transgression. The wish for physical resurrection is thus a regression rather than an advance in religious thinking, a hunger for the lost "good old days" instead of an openness to the mystery yet to be. When we grow dissatisfied with the status quo and ache for something better, past, present, and future can often become ambiguous and entangled. Many moderns, for that reason and others, are not comfortable with a concept of an afterlife that still involves corporeality, and have instead reinterpreted these powerful visions as metaphors for spiritual, not physical, revitalization.

In the Bible, the bliss and serenity of the messianic age is not infrequently preceded by an apocalyptic war. These battles are described in the books of Isaiah, Ezekiel (which contains the famous conflict with Gog and Magog), Joel, Habakkuk, John (in the New Testament), and in many other post-biblical legends. Why would the literary distillations of our yearning for a new, messianic period include such bloody elements? Perhaps they reflect one side of the tension in how human beings try to bring about change. Those who advocate evolution argue that time and patience are essential to achieving our goals; those who promote revolution claim that the old order must be attacked and destroyed before the new one can take its place. The Bible, like human life, is filled with these tensions and conflicting visions, and in its vivid portrayal of the many ways that people respond to their dissatisfaction and restlessness with their present situation, it is a priceless textbook.

————

OUR DESIRE FOR THOSE THINGS we hope will offer meaning and redemption to our lives can be intensely personal. What we yearn for most is not always the actualization of a utopian vision of the future for all of humanity but, rather, a particular situation for our individual life. Abby is a forty-year-old designer. For as long as she can remember, she has wanted to be a parent. "I always thought that our purpose in life is to raise children," she says. Though Abby has always walked her own path, refusing to follow conventional rules or to take on conventional roles, and though she has always been driven by her career, the desire for a child never left her. It gnawed at her. When she turned thirty, Abby decided that by the time she was in her late thirties she would have one. She had several relationships with various men, but none of them worked out. By her mid-thirties, her brother, who'd married earlier, had four children. "Whenever I visited them, and whenever I saw other people's children, I felt deeply sad. It was physical: I actually felt a powerful ache in my arms, my body, my heart."

At about the same time, Abby's best friend died of AIDS. He'd been living in her apartment, and she had cared for him throughout his illness and gradual deterioration. "His death raised a lot of questions for me," she says. "About life. About the kind of life I wanted." Abby was thirty-eight when she finally took concrete steps to have a child. "I didn't want to be fifty and taking my kid to kindergarten. And I didn't want to die without one." Since she did not have a relationship with anyone who seemed like a potential husband or father, she got tested to see if she could conceive and bear a child. "You're not going to have any children," the nurse-practitioner told her flatly. "It was terrible," Abby told me with tears in her eyes. "I had not felt that kind of intense pain since the loss of my best friend. I panicked. I couldn't breathe. I couldn't even talk."

Depressed by her seemingly thwarted desire, Abby gained twenty pounds. She treated being told that she couldn't have a child as a one-two punch. The left jab that dizzied her was having to give up a fantasy of most straight women—namely, getting married to a great guy. But the right cross that toppled her was losing the fantasy of having children. "It was a double whammy," Abby says. "It was hard enough for me to grieve over the first kind of loss. But to mourn the second—that was too much." But then something happened inside her. She said *no,* she refused to accept the situation. "I might have been willing to give up on the first dream, at least for the time being, but I sure as hell wasn't going to give up the second."

Abby started learning about infertility and the various ways of treating it. She read books, articles, surfed the Internet. Adoption had always been an option, but what Abby yearned for most powerfully was a life that was biologically linked to hers, one that developed in her own eggs and emerged from her own womb. The fact that so many factors and forces were aligned against the realization of that goal only seemed to make her want it more. "I felt very much alone during that period," Abby admits. "No one was really able to help me. I had to do it all by myself." It took her two months just to get an appointment to see a physician about possible fertility treatments—one who had more faith in her ability to reproduce than the woman who had earlier (and prematurely) dashed her hopes.

The sperm came from an anonymous donor. Miraculously, Abby got pregnant on her very first attempt. She was ecstatic. Yet after four months, during a business trip, Abby began to hemorrhage aboard an airplane. The hour between the moment she saw blood and the time she landed was the most difficult she can remember. All she could think of was losing the baby. When she arrived and went to a hospital, her worst fears were confirmed by the doctor. After a brief examination, he told her that she had miscarried. The pain at that instant was even more profound for Abby than when the nurse-practitioner had informed her she would never have children. But she didn't believe him. Something within her told her that the baby was alive. She insisted on seeing the sonogram (she had become quite adept at reading the images on the monitor over the previous months). Despite the doubts of everyone around her, Abby detected an image of a beating heart on the screen. That moment, she says, was almost as jubilant as the one when she actually did give birth five months later.

Even that did not take place without struggle. While Abby was in labor, due to an inverted placenta, the baby's umbilical cord became wrapped around its neck. Nevertheless, in the face of multiple and constant obstacles from beginning to end, Abby gave birth to a baby boy. The emotions that had driven her to this point were now matched by emotions of a different kind. "Giving birth was pure joy," she recollects, "the rawest moment you can have in your life. There was nothing intellectual about it." Abby named the baby after her deceased friend. "My boy wanted me as much as I wanted him," she says today. "He chose me, and nothing was going to stop him from entering this world. He has such a strong soul, and part of that soul I know is connected to my friend."

Abby's desire to have a baby gave her the strength to overcome challenges and the faith that she would realize her goal. "I was like a pit bull," she says. "I had my dream in my jaws and I wasn't going to let go of it for anything." Abby has other dreams as well. Though she loves her child more and more every year, she concedes that she would rather share her boy—and her life—with another person: single motherhood is difficult and sometimes lonely. "There's this myth out there that single women have children for companionship," she says. "It's such bullshit. You lose your friends, you lose your whole feminine world, at least for a time. I want it all. But I want it in my own way."

We have seen how people long for the past as well as the future. But is it possible to long for what we already possess? Since yearning is a phenomenon of the heart rather than the head, its manifestations are not always rational. Most of us who have been in love know how feelings of insecurity can arise during the course of a relationship. Sometimes they emerge for good reason (it is the wrong relationship and about to fall apart); sometimes they surface even when everything is going perfectly fine. Our passion for another person can become so intense that we cannot—literally—get enough of that individual. Since a mature relationship is a loving partnership between two separate and autonomous human beings, that desire cannot be continuously satisfied, emotionally or otherwise. And since life is ever-changing and unpredictable, on occasion we fear that our desire will not be filled or reciprocated. This can translate into insecurity about the present. Yet just as some have converted their aching for the past into psalms and lamentations, while others have channeled their craving for the future into messianic visions, men and women have found outlets for their romantic hunger through expressions of love.

There was a debate among the early rabbis on whether to include the Song of Songs in the biblical canon. Some of them found its language too sensual, its imagery too overtly erotic. One of the major reasons that in the end the scroll was included in the Hebrew Bible was that the rabbis interpreted it as a love poem not between a man and a woman but between the Jewish people and God. Whichever is the case, the Song of Songs is a compelling book and a moving expression of passionate love in ancient times. "Let me lean against the stout trunks," one lover says, "let me lie down among the apple trees; for I am sick with love." (2:5) The rapture as well as the disorientation and disease brought on by intense love dates back to antiquity.

Throughout the text, sentiments of confidence are followed by those of insecurity and yearning. "My beloved is mine, and I am his" (2:16) is followed almost immediately with "At night on my bed I sought him whom my soul loves: I sought him, but I did not find him." (3:1) When the female lover finally does find her soul mate (after rising from her bed, roaming the city streets, and soliciting the help of watchmen in her frantic search), she embraces him with what seems as much an expression of her fear of losing him as of joy at being in his presence again: "When I found him whom my soul loves, I held him and would not let him go. . . . " (3:4) In another evocative passage, the lover says, "My beloved put his hand on the latchet of the door, and my heart was excited by him. I rose to open to my beloved; and my hands dripped with myrrh, my fingers with flowing myrrh, upon the handles of the lock." (5:4–5) Yet in the very next verse, her breathless anticipation becomes anxiety and agitation: "I opened to my beloved, but my beloved had turned away, and he was gone; my soul failed when he spoke. I sought him, but I could not find him; I called to him, but he gave me no answer." (5:6)

It appears that constant love is elusive—or at least this particular kind of love. The lover's hunger is never satisfied. She says so herself: "Torrents of water cannot quench love, nor can floods drown it. . . . " (8:7) In romantic love, the sexual component figures prominently. Freud wrote that we must confront "the possibility that something in the nature of the sexual instinct itself is unfavorable to the realization of complete satisfaction." Yet a similar reality exists on the emotional plane. Even when the person we love is an active and pervasive presence in our lives, we can still experience powerful feelings of dissatisfaction and longing. In Plato's *Symposium,* Aristophanes describes the Greek myth of the creation of humanity, which depicts human beings as incomplete creatures perpetually in search of their missing parts. "Love," says Aristophanes, "is simply the name for the desire and pursuit of the whole." Since that cosmic unity is not possible in mortal life, each one of us—like the lover in the Song of Songs—lives in a state of constant yearning for something more than what we have.

I've seen that phenomenon firsthand in my work as the spiritual advisor to a Jewish singles website, Jdate.com. What I try to do through my essays and lectures is stress the importance of having a spiritual foundation—a grounding with God—as a prerequisite to having a healthy, mature relationship with another person. Much of the contact I have with Jdate's members occurs over the Internet. It is there that I have come to see just how difficult it is for single men and women to meet each other in contemporary urban society, and how hard it is to make a relationship work once a couple has started dating. Most of the people I hear from are dissatisfied with their current love lives and hungry for something different, something better.

On a recent book tour, I was able to meet with some members face to face. After I did a reading at a bookstore on the West

Coast, a man about my age came up to me at the signing table. When the others had walked away, he confided to me (in a way that made it seem as if he was almost embarrassed) how frustrated and depressed he was that he couldn't meet the right woman. "I'm a decent-looking guy," he said quietly. "I have a good job, a good lifestyle. What makes it so hard is that I'm *ready*. I really want it, I want to be in love and for someone to love me, and it's just not happening." He proceeded to describe some of his dating horror stories. I could see how much he craved a relationship. And it was clear to me that the human "yearning trait" was only being amplified by the fragmentation and alienation of modern culture. I wasn't sure what to say to him. I felt he mainly wanted me to listen. Part of me wanted to say, "I feel your pain." Another part of me imagined saying, "Look, friend, I'm a Jewish bachelor in his mid-thirties living in New York City. Why the hell are you asking *me* for dating advice?" In the end, all I could say was what he already knew: "It's rough out there."

The feelings that affect the way we view events or institutions also apply to the way we see other people. It is very easy for us to romanticize past relationships, or to create fantasies about future ones. And it is remarkable how quickly we can become dissatisfied with or insecure about the people we are in relationships with. In any of these cases, the same yearning that motivates our behavior can come to stunt it; the same passion that animates our souls can cripple them. Like science and technology, the human heart contains both positive and negative polarities: It can lead us to love or despair, creativity or destructiveness, triumph or disaster.

––––––––

ON ONE LEVEL, popular culture is little more than the primal expression of a society's collective craving. We want to be entertained by movies and music videos, to be fed by McDonald's and Taco Bell, to have our thirst slaked by Budweiser and Pepsi. Today, there also seems to be a deep yearning for what is missing or lost, and it sometimes becomes manifest in popular culture in bizarre ways—the search for Elvis or Atlantis, the shrines to Lady Diana or Jim Morrison. Below the surface, these icons represent something substantial to us, the embodiments of values or dreams we feel in our guts but have trouble articulating: innocence, youth, beauty, perfection. Will there ever be a day when these lost idols come back to us? Will any of them ever satisfy our communal hunger?

For the theist, what we ultimately crave is God. Unlike many other theologians of his time who tried to prove the existence of God using rational arguments, Augustine claimed that the inner hunger that all of us feel is in truth a desire to be united, or reunited, with our Creator. For him, it is the universality and constancy of human yearning that is proof of God's reality. Our yearning is of a kind that no worldly possession or human being could possibly satisfy, and it would not have been implanted in us if it could not be satiated in some other way. That way is God. In Psalm 63, David—who as king has all the power, riches, and lovers he could ask for—is still hungry. But what he hungers for is God, with whom, as we have seen, he has a very fluid relationship: "O God, you are my God; earnestly I seek you. My soul thirsts for you, my flesh longs for you in a dry and thirsty land where there is no water." (63:2) The good news is that God desires to be united with us as well, as Hosea, speaking for God, makes clear: "I will betroth you to me forever; I will betroth you to me in righteousness, in judgment, in love, and in compassion. I will betroth you to me in faithfulness, and you shall know the Lord." (Hosea 2:21–22)

The final satisfaction of all our yearning can seem very distant from our daily lives, and God's presence tremendously elusive. The tension between this promise and our own doubts and fears about it brings us to a crossroads, a turning point not just in this book but in our life's journey. We can desire to escape from the wilderness so badly that, just at the point of finding a way out, we are in danger of taking a more difficult and potentially harmful path. The following two chapters deal with two different routes we can take when we are lost, routes that reflect our having already spent a considerable amount of time and effort wandering in the maze of human experience.

FIVE ANGER

AUSTIN: *I can kill him! I can easily kill him. Right now. Right here.*
All I gotta' do is just tighten up. See? (he tightens cord, LEE
thrashes wildly, AUSTIN releases pressure a little, maintaining
control) *Ya'see that?*
MOM: *That's a savage thing to do.*
AUSTIN: *Yeah well don't tell me I can't kill him because I can. I can*
just twist. I can just keep twisting.

SAM SHEPARD, *True West*

WHEN WE REACH A CROSSROADS, we are faced with having
to choose from among three basic alternatives: going back the
way we came, standing still in a state of paralysis, or picking a
path and moving toward an uncertain destination. But there are
times when *none* of these options seems particularly desirable.
When that occurs, when we have grown weary of our journeying and frustrated with the possibilities that are before us, the
result can be anger. Related to the "flight or fight" response
described so powerfully by Konrad Lorenz is the link between
frustration and aggression. In human beings, in contrast with less
complex animals (where aggression appears to be rooted in an
impulse for self-preservation), the reaction can have an emotional as well as a physical manifestation. None of us likes to be
impeded in his or her progress, unsure which direction to turn.
When Dylan Thomas famously told his father to rage against the
dying of the light, it was a rage that stemmed in part from the
poet's own frustration with the constrictions of mortality.

Randy is a forty-year-old social worker who lives in the Southwest. Though he has worked for nearly two decades in a variety of professional settings, most of his field experience has been with troubled teenagers in urban environments. Two years ago, Randy held a senior position at a government-funded non-profit organization in a major city. Owing to a combination of funding problems and political issues, Randy was forced to lay off two of his case workers. Because all of the other social workers at the organization were already overwhelmed by their own caseloads, Randy had to take over those of his former colleagues himself. Before they left, he asked them if any of their clients were in immediate danger or needed special attention. They said no.

The burden and stress of Randy's work was now compounded. His cases usually involved teenage drug users and dealers, those who had just been released from jail (and who were often angry and extremely violent), and victims of sexual abuse. The small agency was responsible for more than two hundred kids. With the added cases that he inherited from the other social workers, Randy started to feel that he had taken on more than he could handle. Even before the new additions, he wasn't getting much sleep; now he developed a serious sleep disorder. "I spoke with my own counselor about it," Randy said. "But I decided to keep up my work schedule despite my personal problems."

One of the clients Randy inherited was a struggling youth named Scott, a runaway and drug addict who lived in a group home in the area. The counselor who had worked with Scott earlier told Randy not to bother with him. Adhering to the "tough love" philosophy of recovery groups such as Narcotics Anonymous, the former counselor said that the teenager would come to Randy for help when he was ready to receive it. "Now is not the time," he advised Randy. "Let him fall first. He'll get up on his own and find you." Yet Randy tried to develop a relationship with Scott anyway. Randy met with him, his friends, his girl-friend, his fellow drug users. Scott gradually began to trust Randy, to open up to him about his many struggles and problems. "I really felt that we were starting to make some progress," Randy recounts. But he still had dozens of other teenagers to focus on and tend to—he couldn't afford to make any single client an exclusive priority, especially after having been assured by the previous case workers that he needn't be overly concerned with any particular individual.

While Randy was at a hospital one night, he received a call on his cell phone from Scott. It had been an extremely busy evening; Randy was meeting with several clients, some of whom were in detox, and some of whom had recently been admitted for treatment. He'd forgotten an appointment he had made with Scott earlier in the week for that evening. Randy was too involved with the other teenagers to extract himself from the hospital, and told Scott that they would have to reschedule their meeting for another day. Scott seemed disappointed when they finished their conversation. Randy returned to his rounds.

In the morning, after having gotten very little sleep (as usual), Randy's phone rang. It was another social worker. The woman informed him that Scott had died the night before of a drug over-dose. "Scott's dead," the counselor said matter-of-factly. "My first reaction was to tell her to go fuck herself," Randy remembers. "I was so angry. I was mad at the social worker for being so cold, mad at Scott's former counselor for giving me such bad advice, mad at myself for not going with my instincts. I felt that I hadn't worked aggressively enough with Scott, that if I'd been given better information as to the crisis he was really going through, he'd still be alive." Randy started screaming right away, first into the phone and then out loud, alone in his apartment. But the screams soon turned into tears. Randy cried all morning, grieving over the loss of a youth he believed he could have helped more effectively.

Yet anger wasn't the only feeling that Randy experienced after hearing the news of Scott's tragic death. There was also profound guilt: "I'd spent the entire day and night on bureaucratic paperwork," he says, "and with people who were already getting help. What I should have done that night was bolt out of the hospital to see Scott—*he* was the one who really needed me at that moment." Randy was overwhelmed with the horrific conviction that he had made all the wrong decisions and that a disturbed young man he could have saved was now dead. "I was a trained and seasoned professional. I should have been able to hear the desperation in Scott's voice. I wasn't able to do that. I gave him boundaries instead of presence."

Scott's funeral drew more than five hundred wailing teenagers. He had been well known and well liked in his micro-community of troubled youths. Many of the kids were hysterical during the service; a few of them attempted suicide themselves in the days and weeks following the burial. Randy was affected deeply by the whole experience in both conscious and unconscious ways. In the first few days after hearing that Scott had killed himself, he started clenching his teeth at night while he slept (a behavior that continues into the present). The clenching got so bad that he went to an orthodontist and had a device made that he now wears to bed. "I'm sure it has to do with my rage," Randy says. "Well over a year has passed, and I'm still furious about how everything played out."

His frustration and anger showed him that he had lost faith in a system intended to help others, as well as confidence in many of his peers. "In my fury," Randy recounts, "I woke up from my romantic fantasies about the field. I became less accepting of views and opinions that didn't sit right with me, less tolerant of people's laissez-faire attitudes. I still acted like a professional, but I didn't take any shit from anyone. I grew much more forceful and direct in my discussions with colleagues." As a result of his experience, Randy has made the survival needs of his clients his top priority—he refuses to play politics and doesn't care anymore if his choices distance him from his fellow counselors. "I also learned to take care of myself," he says. "I left a situation that had become toxic for me. I accepted a new position and am now much happier. I'm actually starting to sleep again."

————

ANGER IS NOT AN EMOTION WE USUALLY ASSOCIATE with anything beneficial for our souls or for the world around us. But Jung argues that recognizing and accepting the "shadow" aspects of our personality as present and real are essential steps in the path to self-knowledge. These darker kinds of impulses (such as anger, jealousy, and lust) have an *emotional* nature; they are "not an activity of the individual," writes Jung, "but something that happens to him." Since on one level these characteristics represent weaknesses or inferiorities within us, they take place in a lower, almost animalian region—the region of the unconscious. When our shadow breaks through the surface, it is a disturbing but potentially constructive and positive experience, for the shadow is an ambiguous entity, "on one side regrettable and reprehensible weakness, on the other side healthy instinctivity and the prerequisite for higher consciousness."

In Jung's view, many of the classical religious traditions (par-

ticularly Christianity) describe human nature as dualistic, claiming that the shadow dimension of our souls is the source of all
evil. For him, this is a false description. What we call our dark
side consists not only of negative, immoral, or destructive tendencies. It also contains a number of good qualities, such as
appropriate reactions, realistic insights, creative impulses, and
normal instincts. According to Jung, there can be no reality
without polarity. The darkness is as much a part of our lives as
is the light. If channeled properly, our shadow can serve as a
powerful tool for psycho-spiritual development. And trying to
suppress it will never work anyway: "Mere suppression of the
shadow," Jung writes, "is as little of a remedy as beheading would
be for a headache." When Goethe's Faust laments that, "Two
souls, alas, are housed within my breast," he is falling prey to the
unhelpful and unhealthy tradition of artificially splitting our personalities. We each possess only one soul—but it is a soul with
an infinite number of faces.

There is thus an appropriate place in our internal lives for
shadow emotions such as anger. It is what propelled Randy forward in his professional and personal life. It also played a key role
in the lives and work of several significant figures from the Bible.
The prophets first made their appearance in Israel prior to the
establishment of the monarchy. Initially, some of them roamed
the countryside in bands, prophesying in ecstatic frenzies, occasionally to the accompaniment of music. Their role as a kind of
"Pentecostal" subgroup within biblical society was, among other
things, to inspire their fellow Israelites to fight God's holy war
against their Philistine oppressors. (Samuel and Saul, while more
fully developed than other early prophetic figures, fall into this
category.) By the mid–ninth century B.C.E., most likely in reaction to the idolatrous practices of Ahab and a bloody conflict

with the Arameans, ecstatic prophets became especially active. Many lived communally, often in the vicinity of some sacred place and led by a venerated master (Elijah and Elisha are two important examples). These "sons of the prophets" could frequently be distinguished by their dress, and they followed the army into the field.

Yet ancient Israel also had another type of prophet, one who was neither an ecstatic nor a member of a formal community. Instead, he was a solitary individual delivering a message from his God—a message that the recipients often had no wish to hear. The "classical" prophet (such as Isaiah and Micah) lived in the eighth century B.C.E., a period of great prosperity and military strength in both the northern kingdom of Israel and the southern kingdom of Judah. It was also a time, particularly in the north, of social and moral decay. Oppression of the weak, insensitivity toward the impoverished, unethical behavior, infractions of covenant law, and political corruption were common. Pagan practices had infiltrated the national religion. But we hear of no effective protest from the leaders and professional prophets of the day. It was as a result of this void that the classical prophets emerged. No longer ecstatic seers and performers of miracles, these new religious figures served as the conscience of a people, the fiery—and sometimes furious—voices of social justice and spiritual rectitude.

Amos was a shepherd and orchard keeper in Tekoa, a village in Judah just south of Jerusalem. God calls him to be a prophet during the reigns of Jeroboam of Israel and Uzziah of Judah (the rule of the two kings overlapped during the decades from 790 to 750 B.C.E.). Functioning as a mouthpiece for God, Amos castigates the power elite of his era, the leadership in civil and religious life, in commerce and business, in diplomatic and military matters. Their sins have frustrated and angered God, and Amos makes it clear that the fate of the nation hangs in the balance. The judgment upon the southern kingdom: "Because they rejected the law of the Lord, and have not kept his statutes, and their falsehoods have led them astray . . . I will send a fire against Judah and it shall devour the palaces of Jerusalem." (Amos 2:4–5) And upon the northern kingdom: "Because they sell the righteous for silver, and the poor for a pair of sandals . . . and a man and his father go to the same girl, to desecrate my holy name. . . . Indeed, I am creaking underneath you, just as the cart that is full of sheaves creaks." (2:6–7, 13)

God is groaning under the burden of Israel's transgressions. But the breaking point has now been reached, and the divine support that held up the rotting "cart" will not hold anymore—or, more accurately, will be removed. As a consequence of its social injustice and religious apostasy, the house of Israel will tumble, "the archer will not survive, and the swift of foot will not save himself." (2:15) The people are condemned for two reasons: first, for having violated the sacred and eternal covenant with God, and, second, for having closed off the channels of communication *to* God (the text relates how Israel's corrupt leaders have silenced the religious class within their society, ordering the prophets not to prophesy and forcing the Nazirites to break their vow against drinking wine). God is not exacting restitution from Israel because they did not live up to the terms of a contract; God is lashing out at them because they have destroyed an intimate relationship.

The punishments Amos describes are a reflection of the emotions God feels toward the Israelites: "You have built houses of hewn stone, but you shall not dwell in them; you have planted prized vineyards, but you shall not drink their wine." (5:12) But perhaps even worse than physical punishment is divine rejection: "I detest, I loathe your festivals, I have no satisfaction in your solemn gatherings. Whatever you sacrifice to me—your burnt offerings and gifts, your peace offerings and fat cattle—I cannot accept nor approve. Take your loud songs away from me! I will not listen to your instrumental music. But let justice well up as waters, and righteousness as a mighty stream." (5:21–24) We see in this denunciation the depth of God's anger with the Israelites, but we also see a plea for repentance, the only means to escape the impending judgment. In the end, it is their conquest by a foreign power and exile to a foreign land that becomes Israel's fate. Yet, as Amos conveys, it is divine exasperation with a people who have lost their way that sets this national calamity into motion.

While Amos is active in the southern region of the divided kingdom, Hosea is busy excoriating leaders in the north. We know very few personal details about Hosea before he receives the prophetic call (such as what he does for a living or where he is from), but we do know that the call itself involved his private as well as public life. In a divine charge unlike any other in the Bible, Hosea is commanded to marry a woman of questionable character: "At the beginning, when God spoke with Hosea, God said to him, 'Go, take for yourself a promiscuous wife and children of promiscuity, for the land has been promiscuous and strayed from God.'" (Hosea 1:2) Why would God order Hosea to do such a thing? As an Israelite prophet and human channel for the divine word, perhaps God is trying to make Hosea live out what God has already experienced vis-à-vis God's relationship with the (perpetually unfaithful) people of Israel. Whether or not this is "fair" is a separate issue from the probability that his own troubled relationship will give Hosea more profound insight into God's emotions and actions. No wonder some of the prophets try to flee from the divine call.

If the union between God and Israel is being compared to the marriage between Hosea and his faithless wife, Gomer, then the consequences—at least in biblical times—are clear. Israel will receive the same punishment for its behavior that a straying wife deserves. In spite of God's constant care and repeated warnings, Israel has failed to keep her part of the commitment, failed to practice righteousness with one another and fidelity to God. As a result, the chosen people are now threatened with divine repudiation (a rejection that will take the form of military defeat and conquest by a foreign army). This idea is not just communicated through Hosea's words. It is embodied in his *life*. God tells Hosea to name his son *Lo-Ammi,* or "Not My People," since "you are not my people, and I will not be your God." (1:9)

For Hosea, the marriage of God and the people of Israel is consummated during the desert wanderings of the Exodus and corrupted in the settlement of the land of Canaan through Israel's betrayal of God (her "husband") to pursue and romp with other gods (her "lovers"). In the book of Hosea, *promiscuity* and *idolatry* are used as interchangeable terms, and the book's focus shifts back and forth between the deterioration of domestic family life and the same atrophy in the public life (especially in the arenas of religion and politics) of the community as a whole. Hosea's private tragedy is a paradigm for that of Israel, and the rage he expresses toward his adulterous wife mirrors what God feels toward the Israelite leaders and populace who have decided to prostrate their bodies in front of calf statues and embrace the cult of Baal rather than practice monotheism.

God instructs Hosea to confront his "mother" (a euphemism for both the prophet's wife, Gomer, and God's partner, Israel), whom God angrily rejects: "for she is not my wife, and I am not her husband." (2:4) Yet like a heartbroken husband who, despite his pain, is determined to hang on to the one who has deserted him, God holds out a remedy, a possibility for contrition, forgiveness, and reconciliation. But first comes the fury. God tells Hosea to urge the woman to abandon her promiscuous ways, "lest I strip her naked, and set her out as on the day of her birth, lest I treat her as in the wilderness, and deal with her as in the arid land by killing her with thirst. To her children I shall not show pity because they are children of promiscuity." (2:5–6) Clearly, this is the wrath-filled voice of someone (God? Hosea?) whose darker emotions have begun to take possession of him.

The metaphor of relationship makes it easier to understand the connection between Hosea's frustration and the feelings that spill out of him. We often get the most upset at those who are closest to us, particularly if they have let us down or wounded us in some way. How much of the prophet's words are rooted in a sense of righteous indignation, and how much in that of personal conflict, is unclear. What is clear is that, perhaps *because* of the interpersonal component, he still offers his wife/Israel the chance for redemption. If she repents, if she gives up her other lovers, "I shall betroth you to me forever," Hosea says. "I shall betroth you to me with righteousness and with justice, with mercy and with compassion. I shall betroth you to me in faithfulness." (2:21–22) Hosea does not let his anger completely consume him. He argues instead that if trust can be restored to their marriage, the rupture that has brought the relationship to a crossroads can be repaired, and the union between the two might once again be marked by intimacy and affection.

Hosea and Amos, speaking for and sharing emotions with God, use their fury as a means to an end; they do not treat it as an end in itself. The common goal of the two prophets: a moral and sacred society. The fact that such a society always seemed just out of reach does not minimize the power or the urgency of their message.

ROBIN, a fifty-year-old financial planner from Manhattan, recalls an episode that changed her life. "It happened a little over twenty years ago," she says, still uneasy when discussing the event. "I got a call from my mother in the middle of the night. My father had passed out, and an ambulance had taken him to Bellevue, the nearest public hospital. I raced to the emergency room. Walking into Bellevue at three in the morning was like descending into Dante's inferno. The emergency room was filled with drug addicts, the mentally ill, people with gunshot wounds. Sitting next to me was a guy handcuffed to a cop." As she and her mother sat on plastic chairs, Robin learned that her father had suffered a brain hemorrhage and was in a coma.

"The news about my father was traumatizing," Robin says, "but it was traumatizing just *being* there. Every emotion I was feeling got compounded and exaggerated. The staff treated us like criminals—they were functionaries at their worst. The security officers there were all armed. It felt like a lockdown. My mother and I literally camped out in Bellevue. Dealing with the atmosphere, bureaucracy, and bullshit of that place every day for three and a half months wasn't just anxiety-producing. It was infuriating." One morning, a guard was giving Robin a particularly hard time. He wouldn't give Robin and her mother a pass to see Robin's father, who had been placed in an intensive-care unit and who at the time Robin thought might be dying. "I lost it," she remembers. "I just started walking past him. The guard grabbed me from behind, and I exploded. I shouted and made a big scene. I let out all the rage and hatred I was trying hard to contain. I really wanted to hit him. I almost did."

Beyond feeling as if her life was under the control of sadists and misanthropes, the sights, sounds, and smells of the place made Robin—a very sensitive and imaginative person—feel like a prisoner in a concentration camp. "To me," she says, "the guards and staff were the SS, and we were the inmates. Up in the neurosurgery unit, where my comatose father was sprawled out on a gurney and where my emotional state was the most inflamed and chaotic, all of the patients on the floor had shaved heads. People *looked* like inmates in a concentration camp." The experience of both her father's hospitalization and her own inner crisis was shattering: "It was an existential *Kristallnacht*. My entire worldview—moral, psychic, spiritual—was broken into fragments. From the moment I arrived at the emergency room, it was as if I'd entered a different reality, a twilight zone. I was so confused. That feeling of a fractured universe didn't go away after all of it ended. My sensibility about the world never really realigned. I've lived my life since then like a train running over tracks that have been bent, my wheels never quite fitting just right into the grooves."

Visitors were allowed to see patients in the ICU only during certain hours, and for only ten minutes at a time. Yet for Robin, those few moments with her father were themselves oppressive. "There were tubes and wires literally coming out of his head," she recalls. "The only sounds on that floor were the rhythmic hissing of ventilators and the pings of alarms going off." Other than the brief hours Robin and her mother went home to sleep, the two of them essentially lived at Bellevue ("like Gypsies"). Robin's world was a bleak and surreal one, circumscribed by dirty walls and terrible smells, by linoleum and plastic. When she was allowed to be with her father, there wasn't much she could do but hold his hand and look out the one window to the outside world that was near him. "All I could see other than the nightmare I was in was an apartment building across the street from the hospital. There was a swimming pool on top of it. If I turned one way, I saw nothing but disease and desolation. If I turned the other, I saw people *swimming*. It was a completely different world. I couldn't wrap my mind around that incongruity, the disparity of our experiences, separated by just a highway."

In an attempt to reorient herself, Robin (who is Jewish) asked a friend for a prayer book. Since she didn't understand the Hebrew words, Robin looked through it more than she actually read it. But it offered her comfort, and there were times when she was able to pray. "It was my only tangible link," Robin says, "to something other than the bleakness of the world I'd been thrust into." The solace was always short-lived. Her father hovered between life and death during those months: There were times when the chief neurosurgeon was hopeful about his possible recovery and was willing to work hard and commit resources to the effort; at other points, when Robin's father took a turn for the worse, the department chief showed much less interest in the patient. "That man's whim controlled my father's fate," Robin says. As the neurosurgeon grew more unwilling to devote his (or the other attending physicians') attention to her father, Robin and her mother began putting pressure on the chief not to give up. After several days of their intense lobbying, they were asked to come into the neurosurgeon's office. "He let us have it," Robin remembers. "He started yelling and swearing. He said, 'I'm not wasting the resources of this hospital on your fucking father!' Just imagine. Here we were, the man's mother and daughter, already in a state of trauma. And he's cursing at us. He looked at my mother and said, 'Your husband is going to die,' that from then on he wasn't going to allow any medical personnel to enter the room."

Robin's anger toward the doctor transformed into enmity.

She called her brother in Massachusetts the same day and said, "We have to get Dad out of here." Her brother made arrangements for their father to be airlifted from Bellevue to a private hospital in New England. Even if the physicians had given up hope on their father, Robin's family refused to. But her father died that night before the helicopter arrived. "I feel that he ordered my father's death," Robin says of the chief neurosurgeon. "I hate him to this day. And if that place was like a concentration camp, then he was the commandant. He even had a German name."

After her father died, Robin's mother began expressing her own fury—not toward the physician, but toward God. At first, it was very disturbing for Robin. "The hope I found in the prayer book," she says, "the belief that there was a higher being who'd console me, was all rejected by her." Yet Robin soon realized that she wasn't angry like her mother, because as far as Robin was concerned, there now *was* no God: "My mother was enraged, but enraged at something that for her remained real. By that point I was more sad than angry. I mourned the loss of my father, but I also mourned the loss of my belief in God. I desperately wanted to have faith. But it was gone." So was Robin's sense of equilibrium, her capacity to balance her expectations about the world as an orderly and predictable place (a perspective she had learned from her parents) with the harsh reality that it is sometimes just the opposite. "What I lost," she says, "wasn't so much my father as my bearings. Since then, I've gone through life functioning at a very high level, but my feeling of inner direction has always been off."

On the morning of September 11, 2001, two decades had passed since the death of Robin's father. She was in mid-career, with a family of her own. The dust of her earlier trauma had settled. But then terrorists attacked America—with New York at the epicenter of the assault. Robin, who lives in downtown Manhattan, witnessed the collapse of the World Trade Center. She saw (and smelled) the dark plume of smoke dangling ominously over her neighborhood those first few days. She and her family would go outside only with masks over their mouths. She lived through the anthrax scare. All of Robin's deepest fears and most troubling feelings suddenly burst to the surface again.

"The good things I experienced after my father's death," Robin says, "my marriage, a daughter, professional achievement—those things inhabited a separate compartment inside me. But the anxiety and fear of being thrust back into the darkness again were always there, just below the surface, like a low-level hum. On September 11, that darkness wasn't just tapped—it exploded." Robin returned to a place of panic and imbalance; she thought she'd be trapped forever in a world of chaos. She worried about her daughter, fearing that something as terrible as what happened to her father would occur to the girl. Figuring out how to cope with her anger, how to go on in the face of life's fragility and uncertainty, is Robin's great and ongoing challenge, but one she knows she can never really run away from: "Accepting life on its own terms is a constant struggle. I'm not there yet. I'm getting closer, but I'm not yet there. Some people spend their entire lives trying to tear down their illusions. For me, it's the opposite. I need a few of them to keep me from falling."

———

IT ISN'T EASY TO EXPRESS ANGER in a controlled, measured way, and if we lose our grip on it, it can quickly degenerate into something else—hatred. Anger and hatred are often, but not always, interrelated. When the latter takes control of the former, the product in the religious context is usually extremism. This is the fuel that drives inquisitions, crusades, pogroms, and jihads. It is what motivates men to blow themselves up and to take thousands of innocent lives with them. The fury of Amos and Hosea forced their societies to take an honest look at themselves and to improve their behavior. But the hate-filled rage of religious extremists is a mutation from a means to a worthy goal into a dark end in itself, and it can too frequently lead not to social reforms but to anti-social atrocities. The dance between these two powerful forces is a very delicate one, and the more volatile partner sometimes comes out ahead. For Jung, this impulse is a distortion rather than an acceptance of our shadow side, a misinterpretation and misapplication of facts. The shadow emotions become dangerous, Jung writes, only "when our conscious attention to [them] is hopelessly wrong." When it is, those impulses and emotions can produce violent acts that cross the line into questionable and at times even immoral terrain.

In the book of Judges, we find several dramatic figures who seem to hover near that line. The tales about two of them, Ehud and Yael, occur near the beginning of the book. As was noted earlier, the period of the biblical judges was an extremely unstable one, and solid, consistent leadership was a rare commodity but a desperate need. There were struggles with foreign armies as well as between the disorganized Israelite tribes; enmities were bitter, and savage fighting and retaliation were common. The various judges emerged out of this warfare and chaos, only to quickly disappear and leave in their wake a confusion as problematic as before their ascent to leadership positions.

In chapter three, Eglon (a name that means "fat calf"), the Moabite king, defeats the people of Israel and forces them into servitude for eighteen years. An Israelite from the tribe of Benjamin, Ehud ben Gera, devises a plan to avenge his people and punish their conquerors. Ehud journeys to meet Eglon, ostensibly to offer tribute to the king. Ehud, who is left-handed, fastens a double-edged short sword to his right thigh and hides it under his clothes. After presenting his tribute to Eglon, the Israelite informs the ruler that he also has a confidential message for him. Eglon dismisses all of the courtiers and attendants from the royal chamber so that the two men can be alone. Then Ehud approaches the king. "I have a message for you from God," he says. (3:20)

As Eglon rises from his throne, Ehud reaches for the concealed sword with his left hand and plunges it into the king's stomach: "Even the hilt went in after the blade, and the fat closed over the blade, as he did not withdraw the dagger from his belly." (3:21) The fact that Ehud leaves the sword in Eglon's belly suggests that his killing is as much an act of rage as it is one of necessity or justice. While the Bible does not always offer clear expressions of the inner emotions its characters are experiencing, it is often possible (as in the case here) to infer them from outer behavior. Ehud doesn't just slay Eglon—he defiles him. Following the killing, Ehud escapes, rallies the Israelites to wage war against the Moabites, subdues the enemy troops, and becomes a judge over his people until his death. Although Ehud is cast in a heroic light, the text does not say that he was infused with the "spirit of God," as it does with a judge such as Samson. Is this because Ehud has lied and taken God's name in vain? Or because he is too filled with hate to make room for it?

After Ehud's death, the Israelites are again conquered by an enemy, Yabin, king of Canaan. At the time, Deborah is the Israelite judge. She deploys one of her military leaders to do battle against the king's soldiers. The Israelites defeat them, and the commander of the Canaanite army, Sisera, flees for his life. He tries to find refuge in the north in the home of a regional ally. Yael, the ally's wife, says: "Turn here, sir, turn here to me. Do not be afraid."

(4:18) What the commander does not suspect is that Yael is actually sympathetic to the Israelite cause. She invites Sisera into her tent and offers him something to drink (and possibly drugs him). As Sisera dozes on the floor, Yael "took a tent peg, and put the mallet in her hand. She tiptoed in to him. She pounded the peg into his neck and it went into the ground. He had been sound asleep. He twitched convulsively and died." (4:21) Unlike Eglon, who is deceived by an oppressed subject, Sisera is betrayed by a trusted friend. Yet Yael, like Ehud, kills her victim with vigor and (hateful?) passion: She hammers the tent spike with such force that she drives it through Sisera's neck and into the earth.

There are models for this kind of violent behavior that predate the era of the judges. In the book of Numbers, the people of Israel begin "whoring" and worshipping false gods with the Midianites. As Moses and the other tribal heads debate who should punish the ringleaders of these sinful acts, Pinchas, the grandson of the high priest Aaron, summarily executes one of the Israelite men who publicly flouts his people's sacred code with a Midianite woman. After the two of them leave the area near the Tent of Meeting, Pinchas grabs a spear and "followed the Israelite into the chamber and stabbed both of them, the Israelite and the woman, through the belly." (25:8) In a play on words, the Hebrew text could also mean that Pinchas thrusts the spear not through their bellies but "through the private parts." Irrespective of whether Pinchas kills them with wounds to their stomachs or genitalia, he is clearly acting out of profound contempt for the couple. As a result of his execution of the man and woman, God lifts a plague that had been placed on the Israelites as divine retribution for their sins. Yet as one nineteenth-century rabbinic commentator (Samson Raphael Hirsch) observes, had Pinchas not killed them in the act but after the fact, it would have been cold-blooded murder.

More than obvious self-defense killings, the actions of Ehud, Yael, and Pinchas are assassinations. Their actions are motivated not only by political, military, and religious considerations but also—if we are to judge by their methods—by a homicidal disdain for their targets. Deception, betrayal, and heat-of-the-moment eruptions of violence are all elements that reflect not just the discharge of one's duty but expressions of scorn. This is the borderline where anger crosses over into enmity, where the shadow can become a death shroud. As we know from history and current events, it is always risky when societies or governments act out of the perceived need for vengeance, retaliation, or punishment. Sometimes the victims slide into the role of oppressors. Are the above early figures simply less mature in dealing with their indignation than later ones such as Amos and Hosea?

Ehud, Yael, and Pinchas may behave in ways that raise some serious questions, but in the biblical context they are nevertheless trying to defend their people as well as their spiritual traditions and laws. In the case of a later prophet, Elisha, we find an example of someone who does neither, whose spasm of rage and violence appears unjustifiable by any measure. In the second book of Kings, the great prophet Elijah is near the end of his divine mission. As his disciple Elisha converses with him by the Jordan River, a chariot of fire, pulled by horses of fire, suddenly materializes in the sky, swoops down in between the two men, and carries Elijah "up by a whirlwind into heaven." (2:11) There is no epilogue, no death scene. Elijah just vanishes, literally, into thin air. In a ritual (and perhaps perfunctory) act of mourning, Elisha rips off all his clothes. Then, in the very next instant, he jumps at the opportunity to fill the vacuum in prophetic leadership.

Picking up Elijah's fallen mantle from the ground, Elisha stands by the bank of the Jordan. He strikes and divides the water, calling out, "Where is the Lord, the God of Elijah?" (2:14) After the waters have parted, exposing dry land for him to cross, the text tells us that Elisha "went over." But as the rest of the story suggests, the territory he enters exists on more than just the material plane. Although both Elijah and Elisha are prophets in the "ecstatic" mold (and frequently depicted performing or associated with supernatural phenomena), only Elisha seems to walk on the dark side of spirituality and moral behavior. The prophet and his disciple enter two entirely different metaphysical regions: Elijah, a kind of messianic figure in the Jewish tradition, goes up; Elisha, a murkier character, goes *over*. One enters the kingdom of heaven, the other a netherworld of shadows.

There is no question that Elisha has inherited from his teacher many wondrous and powerful abilities—the problem is how he uses them. Perhaps the most horrifying and violent example of how the prophet misuses his supernatural talents occurs in almost a side note at the outset of his spiritual vocation. As Elisha is traveling to Bethel, he encounters a band of small children who run up from behind and begin to make fun of him: "Go up, you bald head! Go up, you bald head!" (2:23) Enraged, Elisha turns back, glares at them, and curses the children in God's name. Then, mysteriously, magically, and implicitly by the prophet's own hand, "two she-bears emerged from the wood and tore apart forty-two of the children." (2:24) After this gruesome slaughter, Elisha continues on his journey without a word. In this single episode, Elisha blatantly violates two of the Ten Commandments: He takes God's name in vain and murders innocent people. Not just "people" in the generic sense but *little children*. Elisha's fury and hate take possession of his soul. What he displays is not immorality but evil. He kills not to defend a nation or a faith but because he is offended by a bunch of kids.

———————

ANGER IS A SLIPPERY EMOTION. What might begin as a justified, moderate reaction to a personal affront or an act of injustice can suddenly cascade into something far more sinister. And when outrage gets mingled with hatred, the result can be lethal. Sometimes these expressions of rage are rooted in issues that have little or nothing to do with the situation or object at hand. While I was living in Jerusalem as a college student, I spent a weekend with an Israeli friend, Igal, in a development town in the north. Igal, whose parents came to Israel from Morocco during a wave of North African Jewish immigration in the 1950s, introduced me to a friend of his from the same army unit. It was a Saturday afternoon, the heart of the Jewish Sabbath.

The young soldiers did not like coming home on the weekends. Their households, like many of the other ones in the town, were far more repressive than the free and easy lifestyles they were living on the outside (at least when they were on leave from their military posts). Their families observed a rigid form of traditional Judaism that they had brought over from Morocco, and it made the two men—secular Israelis who viewed themselves as free of the rules of religion—feel trapped, especially on the Sabbath. But Igal had learned to cope with this generation gap, and with the fact that he'd had a restrictive upbringing. His friend responded to the discomfort differently. After lunch, the three of us walked into the woods near their neighborhood. I followed them to a shed. Igal's army buddy, a short, sinewy infantryman with wild eyes that never looked straight at you, approached the shed by himself. I heard squealing coming from inside it. As he entered, the squealing grew louder and more piercing. Within a few seconds, Igal's friend reappeared with a sack hung over his shoulder that contained something the size of a small dog. It was squirming and still squealing, but the sound was muffled.

Igal and I followed him to a tree stump a few yards away from the shed. There was a large knife on top of it. The friend reached into the sack and pulled out a baby pig. With no burlap to serve as a barrier, the pig's crying rang through the woods. It sounded like a human scream, and it didn't stop until the soldier had placed the animal on the stump and started to slit its throat with the knife. Then the scream turned into a hideous gurgle—he'd begun his butchery at the wrong spot, severing not the artery that would have killed it quickly but cutting instead into the soft tissue and muscle. The baby pig writhed helplessly, still fully conscious, blood spraying from its neck as its head became more detached from its body. I will never forget its eyes or that gurgle. When he had finally sliced all the way through the bone, the noise ended abruptly and the pig's tiny head fell to the ground. Igal's friend tossed it casually into a bush.

I stood there stunned as he butchered it, presumably to be eaten at some future meal away from his family. Though the soldier's face remained relatively calm throughout the whole episode, it was hardly lost on me that this young Israeli had slaughtered a pig—an animal that in Judaism is expressly forbidden from being eaten—on a Jewish holy day. What I had witnessed was not an accidental act but a deliberate, perhaps unconscious *desecration,* an angry and violent lashing out at the man's parents, the religious traditions they embraced, and the God they believed in. The poor pig had the misfortune of being caught in the middle of it all; it had become more a metaphor than a living being. And the tree stump on which the baby pig was killed had been transformed into an altar of loathing.

These examples vividly illustrate that the wellsprings for

our anger are multiple and varied: a need to rebel, a sense of moral indignation, a feeling of frustration. Yet as Lorenz implies and Jung states clearly, the same primitive, shadow emotions that have their legitimate place—and even useful function—in our lives can be hard to rein in once they have been unshackled. An appropriate relationship with the darker aspects of our personalities can lead to self-knowledge, self-acceptance, and the cathartic defusing of our negative energy. It can even lead to an improvement in the conditions of other people. But an inappropriate one, grounded in misunderstanding or misuse, can make us lose our way—psychologically, morally, and spiritually. And when hatred seeps into the dynamic, when our personal animus causes us to demonize others, we can act reprehensibly. In reaction to our frustration and pain, we often want to assign blame. *What bastard placed me in this predicament?* Sometimes we feel that way toward God. We feel marooned, abandoned, rejected. Yet no amount of rage or enmity will help to answer our questions or extricate us from our quagmires.

It isn't easy to separate the internal issues that motivate us from the external forces that affect us as well. But progress comes with a price: struggle. Anger, even when appropriate, should never be more than a middle step, a way station on our pilgrimage. When it becomes an end in itself rather than a means to one, the consequence can be a deadening stasis. Those who succumb to that darkness remain (or become) lost. Those who refuse to give in to it, who resolve with all their hearts and souls to move forward despite their own difficulties and challenges, are the courageous ones who gain a glimpse of the horizon ahead.

SIX DETERMINATION

I was struck with the singular posture he maintained. Upon each side of the Pequod's quarter deck, and pretty close to the mizzen shrouds, there was an auger hole, bored about half an inch or so, into the plank. His bone leg steadied in that hole; one arm elevated, and holding by a shroud; Captain Ahab stood erect, looking straight out beyond the ship's ever-pitching prow. There was an infinity of firmest fortitude, a determinate, unsurrenderable wilfulness, in the fixed and fearless, forward dedication of that glance.

HERMAN MELVILLE, *Moby-Dick*

WHILE ANGER IS AN EXPRESSION OF THE HEART, determination is an act of the will. After having confronted (and hopefully worked through) our feelings of loneliness, pain, and rage at being lost, we can arrive at a point where we resolve to break free of the forces that are holding us back or harming us in some way. As is the case with many of the stages we have explored in this book, there is an element of risk that is always present whenever we venture out into the unknown. Sometimes those journeys will take place in the company of others; much of the time we will experience them alone. Yet individual initiative is often the key to our success, at times even to our survival. As the Jewish sage Hillel states, "If I am not for myself, who will be for me?"

From his firsthand observations as a concentration-camp prisoner in Dachau and Buchenwald, Bruno Bettelheim concluded that the inmates who gave up and died were those who had also given up any attempt to act with personal autonomy, who had succumbed to their captors' goal of dehumanizing and exercising absolute control over them. In Bettelheim's view, even the smallest and seemingly most insignificant expressions of the individual will—for example, a prisoner deciding whether to eat a piece of bread he or she is given or save it for future consumption—can make the difference between life and death. When a Paraguayan rugby team's plane crashed in the Andes (their harrowing story was made famous by the book *Alive*), stranding them without proper clothing or enough food to survive, it was not the strongest or most athletic members of the squad who made it out alive but, rather, the ones who refused to give up hope.

Though most of us will never have to go through the experiences described above, we all face hardships during the course of our lives. Yet it frequently takes a challenging event or arduous episode to demonstrate just how resolute our wills actually are. Anthony is a graphic designer in his mid-thirties who lives in New England. He grew up in a highly sheltered environment, the only child of Italian-American parents. His mother was a very strong and domineering woman, and since his father was hardly ever home, Anthony's experience growing up as a child was extremely unpleasant. He remembers that from an early age he would ask himself questions about life, meaning, God. But he had nobody to discuss them with nor an outlet through which to vent them. By the time he was eleven, Anthony had started to use drugs and alcohol.

He ran away from home in his late teens, traveling through Western Europe before settling in Madrid. "I was searching for truth," Anthony recollects, "as much as I was looking for a community." He arrived in Madrid with a few dollars in his pocket and a crumpled slip of paper that an American friend had given him when he left home. Scribbled on it were the name and telephone number of a person Anthony could contact if he needed help. After staying at a youth hostel for a few nights (he worked as a dishwasher and cleaner in exchange for his bunk bed), Anthony called his friend's contact, a Spanish college student, and slept on the floor of his apartment for another week. But the arrangement didn't work out, and soon Anthony was again without a home. Over the next five years, Anthony took odd jobs and slept at hostels, with acquaintances, in stairwells and cafes. "I'd become homeless," he recounts. "I went in and out of apartments and jobs during that time like they were revolving doors. I once calculated them all—thirty-seven different places. I was also drinking and drugging, and that became heavier and heavier as the years went by."

Anthony says now that he was a wayward soul, but back then, because he was in a fog and numbed much of the time, he didn't really feel it. Yet one morning, as he was walking to a market, Anthony was jolted into consciousness: "A guy in front of a tobacco shop called me over. I can't really remember what he wanted. I walked across the street, and suddenly I heard an explosion behind me. I turned around and saw a car in flames. Everyone was stunned. Then, within seconds, I saw a flash of light and heard another, even louder blast. About half a block away, I saw bodies and blood flying through the air. A cell of Basque separatists had set off two bombs."

The experience shook Anthony to his core. It showed him how much anger there was in the world, and also in his own heart. Anthony was angry at everything—at his mother, for pushing him away and (in his mind) putting him in his present situation; at the people he knew in Madrid, who he thought were using him for his access to drugs; at himself, for falling into homelessness, poverty, and isolation. At that point, Anthony decided to write off God as well as everybody around him. To channel and fend off his feelings of hopelessness and at times suicidal despair, he wrote poetry. But it wasn't enough. He sensed he needed help, and as a first step toward straightening himself out, he enrolled in an AA program.

The meetings were worthwhile, but it was not until Anthony became friends with another troubled American that he was able to take the second step toward extracting himself from his existential muck and mire. The young woman with whom he became friends also had a drug problem. Although Anthony had been a loner in Madrid until the two of them met, they decided to live together (in a strictly platonic way). They were both still homeless, but for the next eight months Anthony and his friend offered each other companionship and mutual support. "On the street," he says, "you need to have someone who's watching your back." His friend's drug use intensified, and Anthony worried that she might not make it. As a person who always attempted to help other people even when he didn't take care of himself, Anthony tried to serve as a role model for her. He resolved to get off drugs cold turkey, and it was his desire to assist his friend that gave him the inner fortitude to do it. Anthony made her join a substance-abuse program with him. For a time, it worked: He got clean, and her drugging diminished significantly.

The young woman eventually returned to the States. Anthony, now alone again for the first time in nearly a year, began to deteriorate. Following several relapses, he was kicked out of the rehab program. The counselors arranged for him to move into a hostel, where he slept on the roof and had to do dishes and other chores to pay his way. Anthony was back where he'd started from—he had come full circle. At a July 4 party with other Americans who were staying at the youth hostel, he figured that if he was careful he could participate in their celebration. But before long, Anthony had swallowed a handful of pills and most of a bottle of whiskey. "There was a ledge on the roof where we were partying," he says. "I don't really remember what happened exactly. Somebody might have tripped me or pushed me. But the next thing I knew, I had fallen off the ledge to the ground below. It was a couple of stories high, I think. I hit my head on the concrete—I'm surprised I didn't get killed. They called an ambulance, and I got rushed to the hospital."

Anthony had hit rock bottom. After several days of medical care and recuperation, and before his doctor said he was ready to be discharged, Anthony simply walked out of the hospital, the bandages still wrapped around his skull. With no money, he had to panhandle to get bus fare back to the hostel. "I looked like a monster," he recalls. "Dried blood on my forehead. Torn clothing. I was a total mess." Anthony settled into life at the hostel again, but the staff there kept a constant eye on him. He did his work and kept to himself, rarely interacting with the teenagers and college students who passed in and out of the building. A few months later, however, Anthony met a pretty Italian woman. They struck up a conversation and became friends. Then they decided to travel to Toledo together for a weekend. By the time the two of them returned to Madrid, they had fallen in love and had become inseparable.

"From that point on, I worked my ass off," says Anthony. "We wanted to move in together, so between the two of us we managed to scrape together some money and found a cheap flat near the hostel." His love for his girlfriend helped him to steer clear of drugs and alcohol; though she told him that she accepted him as he was, he knew he would lose her if he began using them again. The couple lived together for six months, and for Anthony it was the happiest period of his years abroad. But his girlfriend needed to return to Italy for school. They both decided to try to continue the relationship. "There were only two things I was focused on then," he says. "The first was leaving Madrid—if I stayed, I knew I'd fall back into the same destructive pattern and never get out of that place alive. The second was seeing her. Even after finally making it back to the United States, I was determined to see her every six months, come hell or high water. And to stay clean."

That is what he has done. Anthony reconciled with his mother (they hadn't spoken in almost two years when he first contacted her to say he was coming home). He lives with her now in his old house, goes to AA meetings, and is enrolled at a trade school. He and his girlfriend trade off visits to each other's country. "I feel like a different person," Anthony says. "It's still a daily struggle not to have a drink or to take drugs, and who knows for sure if our relationship will survive, but right now I feel like I've come out the other side of a nightmare. This was my third step, and this time it's for real. Now I want to straighten myself out for no reason or person but *me*."

———

THE BIBLICAL NARRATIVE OF TAMAR is the story of one woman's bold and determined effort to singlehandedly transport herself from a place of personal loneliness and social marginality to a new, more hospitable position. Toward the end of the book of Genesis, we learn that Judah, the patriarch of one of the Israelite tribes, has arranged for the marriage of his firstborn son, Er, to Tamar, a Canaanite woman. Yet Er dies soon after the union, so Judah arranges for the widowed Tamar to marry a second son, Onan (in accordance with the ancient practice of levirate marriages). He too dies, leaving Tamar a widow once again. With only his youngest son, Shelah, remaining, "Judah said to his daughter-in-law Tamar, 'Stay as a widow in your father's house until my son Shelah grows up'—for he thought, 'He too might die like his brothers.'" (38:11) Judah orchestrates the removal of Tamar from his house—perhaps because he doesn't want to test fate on one of his children a third time, or perhaps to make Shelah's obligation to marry her less pressing. Regardless of Judah's true motivation, Tamar obeys the instructions of her father-in-law and waits patiently for his son to mature. But years pass, Judah's own wife dies, and still we hear nothing of his earlier commitment to Tamar.

In biblical society, being a single woman of marriageable age (and, worse, a widow with a checkered history) was, to put it mildly, unpleasant. Israelite culture was clan-centered, and living without a family of one's own could be viewed with suspicion and lead to alienation or ostracism. Refusing to accept her problematic situation, Tamar resolves to get what she wants—a husband, a father to have children with, a way to connect with others and participate in her community. Like her father-in-law, she devises a plan to bring about her desired goals. And she won't stop until she achieves them.

Tamar learns that Judah is traveling to the town of Timnah for the seasonal sheep-shearing and its attendant festivities. Setting her plot into motion, Tamar "took off her widow's garb, covered her face with a veil, and, wrapping herself up, sat down at the entrance to Enaim, which is on the road to Timnah; for she saw that although Shelah had grown up, she had still not been given to him as a wife." (38:14) By taking off her widow's clothes, Tamar is doing more than preparing to put on a disguise—she is throwing off a life that was forced on her. Wearing a veil also does more than simply shield her identity; in the context of the time, the appearance of a woman dressed as Tamar waiting alone along the route to Timnah would have been a tempting diversion to lonely male travelers away from home. When Judah passes through Enaim, he takes the veiled Tamar to be a prostitute and propositions her.

Tamar asks what he will pay her to sleep with him. Her unsuspecting father-in-law offers her a kid from his flock. Tamar accepts the barter arrangement but demands that Judah leave a pledge with her until he sends her the kid (something he can't exactly pull out of his pocket and give her on the spot). Judah asks Tamar what kind of a pledge she wants. "She replied, 'Your seal-and-cord, and the staff which you carry.' So he gave them to her and slept with her, and she became pregnant by him. Then she went on her way. She took off her veil and again put on her widow's garb." (38:18–19)

With Judah now ensnared in her trap (which clearly involved meticulous planning as well as personal risk), Tamar returns home. After Timnah's sheep-shearing festival concludes, Judah sends a friend of his to deliver the bartered kid to and retrieve his pledge from the prostitute in Enaim. But the man cannot find her there. He inquires of the residents in town as to her where- abouts, yet no one knows of any prostitute who has been in the area. The man goes back to Judah and informs him about the results of his search. Rather than making another attempt to find the mysterious woman, and perhaps weighing the alternatives of either following through on his debts or running around the countryside trying to track down a harlot, Tamar's father-in-law decides that it is probably better just to drop the whole thing: "Judah said, 'Let her keep them, lest we become a laughing- stock.'" (38:23)

Three months later, Judah receives word that Tamar has pros- tituted herself and become pregnant. He orders for her to be dragged from her home and burned alive (out of fury or because she has committed a capital crime, adultery, since she is still technically engaged to Judah's son and the biblical laws of adultery applied to engaged as well as married people). As she is brought out to be executed, Tamar sends a covert message along with the pledge items that have been in her possession to her father-in-law, informing him that the man by whom she has been impregnated is the same one to whom the items belong: "And she added, 'Examine these, the seal-and-cord and the staff—whose are they?' Judah recognized them and said, 'She is more in the right than I, inasmuch as I did not give her to my son Shelah.' And he was not intimate with her again." (38:25–26)

Judah's epiphany that he has unjustly prevented Tamar from moving on with her life, and getting what she was entitled to by tradition and law, is the direct result of Tamar's patient determination, her willingness to use unorthodox and hazardous methods to defy her lot and wrest from those around her a situation and station more tolerable to her. As the mother of his future children (she will have twins), Tamar is now considered Judah's wife, though her previous relations with his sons make further intimacy between them undesirable. Judah, without much of an option—and possibly even against his own will—takes the place of his son. And although Tamar's marriage may not be filled with the affection and love most of us strive for today in our unions with others, she has largely achieved her goals: a path out of isolation and participation in her society.

Tamar shares some important similarities with another compelling female character from the Bible, Esther. Familiar to Jews through the joyous holiday of Purim, Esther is the heroine who saves her community from the anti-Semite Haman, an advisor to the Persian royal court who plots to have the Jewish people destroyed. Through a combination of deception (Esther initially hides her Jewish identity) and sexuality, Esther sets into motion a counterplot, manipulates the king, and foils Haman's murderous plan. As the Genesis narrative illustrates, Tamar also utilizes deception and sexuality to manipulate a powerful male figure and achieve her own ends. But there is a key difference between the two women. Esther may be the better known of the pair, but her activities are directed mostly behind the scenes by her uncle Mordechai. Tamar, on the other hand, strategizes and acts without any outside help or support, and it is only through her clandestine machinations and fortitude that she is saved from a life of misery.

———

THERE ARE SOME CHALLENGES, however, in which the assistance and support of others is essential. Diane, a caterer in her late forties, faced that kind of challenge after the birth of her first child. "There is no preparation for parenting," she says. "It is incredibly hard and stressful work, and when you have a child who is especially difficult, then all of those struggles get exacerbated." Diane's first child, a son, took over her life. While her husband worked, Diane was left more or less alone to deal with a boy who was "very active and physical, easily explosive, hypersensitive to touch, extremely curious, articulate, volatile, and clingy." This wide array of personality traits and behaviors would have made him a tremendous challenge for any seasoned parent, but for Diane he was overwhelming.

"As a mother," Diane says, "his problems hurt me deeply. I was so frustrated at not being able to understand my child's difficulties and not being able to soothe him. The situation also created a great deal of anxiety in and put pressure on our family life. His mood in the morning affected how everyone's day evolved. I never dreamed that having a temperamental child could produce such stress. I remember waking every morning with a knot in my stomach, not knowing what the day would bring." Sometimes Diane would go through the morning "without breathing" until her son was delivered to school. Then she would sit in a chair and take several deep breaths to help herself relax. During the afternoon she would try to do "something nice" for herself, such as meeting a friend for lunch, exercising, going shopping, or just spending some quiet time at home. On the days that she worked, Diane would often be distracted from the tensions of raising her son.

Diane made it her focus to try to understand her son, to provide him with the help he needed to channel his energies and calm his explosiveness so that he could grow and develop in a healthy way. "Despite loving him enormously," Diane recounts, "I was always on edge, never knowing when the next meltdown would occur. It could be in the middle of the supermarket, in the street, at Thanksgiving dinner, at his friend's birthday party, in school, or at home when I didn't get the right snack." Diane was eventually able to read certain indicators from her son and know when to end a play date, when not to go out to dinner, when to eliminate an errand. "In time, fathoming why life was so hard for this little person became less important to me than constructing strategies to help quell the eruptions," she says.

Along with her husband, Diane actively sought the help of others. They developed a support system of family, friends, teachers, tutors, and therapists (both traditional and alternative). "The challenge for me as a parent," she says, "was to step back, to refrain from my impulse—which was to jump in and try to defuse—and *guide* rather than intervene. My test as a mother was to maintain confidence while being directed, not by absolute certainty and total self-reliance but by instinct, information I had collected, trial and error, and understanding friends and professionals." Occasionally, someone in her family would comment that Diane was being inconsistent or too permissive. One close relative suggested that she leave her son with him for a few days—he'd whip him into shape. Diane recalls one painful conversation with an aunt "when she politely told me not to bring my child to a family dinner because he might be disruptive. I contained my anger and said that if his behavior disintegrated I would leave, but that if we came to the dinner at all we were coming as a family. The event went well, but it was difficult for me to enjoy myself because I was on alert the whole evening."

Having a support system allowed Diane to feel as if she were part of a community, and kept at bay the loneliness that she would sometimes experience during particularly difficult moments. "Following a stressful situation," she says, "I could call several people for support and comfort. I knew there was always someone available to get me through a tough time. I didn't always know what I was doing, but I trusted my instincts. At times I would feel like this was some kind of ordeal, and though I couldn't figure out its purpose, I had faith that we would come out of it okay." Despite her optimism, Diane became envious when she observed other mothers with easier children and calmer lives: "But then I would have this wonderful parenting moment, and I'd feel pleasure and pride. The ups and downs weren't a source of stability, but they provided a richness I wouldn't have had if my child was less challenging."

Diane intermittently questioned her ability as a parent. She wanted her son to fit in and not stand out, yet she frequently had to push beyond that desire in order to meet her child's needs. "It was uncomfortable for me," she says, "to have to leave a situation because of poor behavior, and it was hard not to lose sight of the fact that it had nothing to do with me, that it was my child's reaction to a specific event or context. I often felt embarrassed and a need to explain. Sometimes I wished I could be strong enough to just walk away and not care about what people thought. But I was determined to succeed as a parent and mother. I was unwavering in my goal of making things right for my child."

As Diane's son grew, he gained more control over his impulsive outbursts. He had fewer incidents, and there was more tranquillity in the household. The morning anxiety largely disappeared. When a tense situation did occur, the anxiety would come back as well. But Diane had developed effective coping mechanisms—deep breathing, calling up friends or counselors—to help her get through it. "It wasn't just the result of my efforts alone," she says, "that my son has reached the point he's at today: calmer, more grounded, healthy. It took many adults to get him there. And he put enormous effort into it himself. The aunt who asked me not to bring him to dinner is now one of his biggest fans and a great support to me. Several of the teachers who stuck with us continue to check in. It took a community to overcome the obstacle of parenting a challenging child."

Diane no longer questions her abilities as a parent. She knows she made some poor decisions but also many correct ones. Her son is now a senior in high school and getting ready for college, and when on occasion he has another "meltdown," she is not overwhelmed by it. Through her love, devotion, and stalwart efforts, Diane survived the crucible of parenthood. Yet it might not have happened nearly as successfully had she lacked the wisdom to recognize her limitations and the humility to permit others to counsel and assist her.

———

THE SUPPORT OF OTHERS can be vital to our efforts to surmount the challenges we face in our lives, but ultimately we alone are the final arbiters of the paths and strategies we choose (even if one of those choices is *in*action or despair). Jean-Paul Sartre says that we are "condemned" to this freedom; others would say that it is in the decision-making process itself—the shadow land where nothing is certain and all is possible—that human beings find their greatest nobility. But for that freedom not to wither and die, it must be exercised, like a muscle, over and over again. Every waking moment presents us with multiple alternatives, a labyrinth of options. How we confront and respond to them shapes our souls and directs our steps, as well as the steps of those who follow us.

Abraham faces his own call to action in the Mesopotamian town of Haran, a name that means *crossroads*. Not only does the biblical patriarch (a holy figure in Judaism, Christianity, and Islam) receive the divine call at the crossroads of his life—he receives it at a turning point in the Bible itself. Abraham has been referred to as the first major historical figure in the book of Genesis. Unlike Adam or Noah, who seem to serve as symbolic representations woven into primeval memories and myths, Abraham appears not as a persona but as a *person,* an identifiable human being who lives in a specific place and at a certain time. Is his personality, his humanity, the result (or the reward) of the actions that he takes? What we do know is that God selects Abraham to fulfill a sacred mission, to set into motion the wheels of a destiny that continues to unfold. God gives Abraham (known at this point in the tale as Abram) a charge: "Go forth from your native land, and from your father's house, to the land that I will show you. And I will make of you a great nation, and I will bless you." (12:1–2)

Abraham does not have to accept the mission. Some of the characters who precede him in the Bible run away from such celestial charges. Why does God remind Abraham that he must give up so much—his homeland, his hearth, his way of life—if he is to venture into terra incognita? Why doesn't God simply say, "Go to the land that I will show you," without any prefatory comment? Perhaps to imply that what Abraham is about to embark on is less a trip than a trial, a test, an ordeal—the first of several that the patriarch must encounter and pass through during the course of his life. The blessings that Adam and Noah receive from God are gifts; the blessing that Abraham receives is conditional, in that he and his progeny must embrace and observe the obligations of their eternal covenant with God in exchange for the bounty they are to reap. Abraham accepts the charge and begins his pilgrimage, roving from Mesopotamia to Canaan, from Canaan down to Egypt, and then from Egypt back to the Promised Land. The fact that Abraham resolves to give up everything that is comfortable and familiar for the ambiguity of a promised but as yet unrealized future offers a taste of the fortitude he will demonstrate more clearly later in the narrative.

In chapter 18 of Genesis, Abraham learns that God is preparing to destroy the cities and residents of Sodom and Gomorrah in punishment for their moral and spiritual crimes. He confronts God directly and questions the divine plan: "Abraham came forward and said, 'Will you sweep away the innocent along with the guilty? What if there should be fifty innocent within the city; will you then wipe out the place and not forgive it for the sake of the innocent fifty who are in it? Far be it from you to do such a thing, to bring death upon the innocent as well as the guilty, so that innocent and guilty fare alike. Far be it from you! Shall not the judge of all the earth deal justly?'" (18:23–25)

Talk about guilt trips! Abraham utilizes that weapon, as well as those of logic and merciful compassion, in a concerted effort to dissuade God from going ahead with the annihilation. If God allowed a saving remnant after the Flood (largely because of the righteousness of Noah), why not apply the same rationale to the twin cities of sin? And if God tested Abraham in chapter 12, then their roles are reversed here—Abraham is testing *God's* consistency and fairness, the parameters of the divine value system, his Creator's capacity for grace. God agrees not to wipe out the population if fifty innocent people can be found. In a masterfully manipulative strategy to curry divine favor before further negotiations, the text tells us that "Abraham spoke up again, saying, 'Here I am presuming to speak to the Lord, I who am but dust and ashes: What if the fifty innocent should lack five? Will you destroy the whole city for want of the five?' And God answered, 'I will not destroy it if I find forty-five there.'" (18:27–28)

Abraham's humble and self-deprecating words mask a resolute and tenacious will. Like a pit bull, the patriarch latches onto the argument that has led to God's qualification (or retreat) and will not let go. He asks God if the same would apply if forty innocent people could be found, and God says the city will still be spared for the sake of the forty. Then Abraham continues, "Let the Lord not be angry if I go on: What if thirty should be found there?" (18:30) God agrees to spare it for the sake of the thirty. As a result of his skills as a negotiator and his refusal to take no for an answer, Abraham is able to whittle down the number of innocents who would redeem the other residents of the city to just ten, at which point the negotiations cease. Yet not even those ten individuals can be discovered in antiquity's most notorious den of iniquity, and the denizens of Sodom and Gomorrah are soon consumed by sulfurous fire that falls from heaven.

Abraham's tenacity and determination come into play later in the Genesis narrative as well. In a story known as the Akedah, or "the Binding," Abraham attempts to offer his son Isaac as a sacrifice to God. He does this not because the patriarch *wants* to but because it is what God commands him to do—it is an act of will, not an expression of desire. And since the text makes it clear how much Abraham loves his son, his outer actions may very well stand in stark opposition to his inner emotions. After a three-day journey, Abraham reaches the divinely designated location where the sacrifice is to take place. He builds an altar, lays out the firewood, binds Isaac, and lifts the knife. At that moment, "an angel of the Lord called to him from heaven: 'Abraham! Abraham!' And he answered, 'Here I am.' And he said, 'Lay not your hand against the boy, nor do the least thing to him. For now I know that you fear God, since you have not withheld your own beloved son from me.'" (22:11–12) Abraham spots a ram that is caught in a nearby thicket, and the animal is sacrificed instead of Isaac.

This biblical tale has raised many questions from innumerable thinkers for centuries, but one thing that is never questioned is the resolve that Abraham demonstrates as he tries to carry out God's order. When the patriarch responds to the angel's call with the phrase "Here I am," he is using a Hebrew word (*hineni*) that has a coded meaning in the rabbinic tradition. For the rabbis, *hineni* is a signifier that indicates a person of moral and spiritual integrity, someone who is ready and able to do God's will. It is a word uttered by figures such as Jacob, Moses, Samuel, and Isaiah, an expression meant to convey commitment and fidelity to their sacred calling.

Yet that extreme commitment can sometimes have unsettling consequences. Rashi, the great medieval commentator and redactor, was curious about a different part of the exchange above. Why does the angel add a seemingly superfluous phrase ("nor do the least thing to him") to its injunction to Abraham? For Rashi and other rabbis of the period, nothing could be accidental or unnecessary in the Torah, the infallible manifestation of God's mind and will. He cites a midrash to explain the additional phrase: "Abraham said to God, 'If this be so [the fact that Isaac does not have to be sacrificed after all], I have come here in vain. Let me at least inflict a wound on him and draw some blood from him.' God replied, 'Nor do the least thing to him.'" According to this interpretation, Abraham is so determined to fulfill the divine charge that even after the command itself has been annulled, he seems unable to stop himself. The extra phrase represents God's intervention, an attempt to prevent the overly fervent (frenzied?) patriarch from harming his son.

Determination, like most other experiences and attributes, has a dark side. The zeal that can lead to blessing can also warp into *obsession,* producing ugly, sometimes fatal outcomes. To take a literary example, Captain Ahab's relentless, fierce resolve to hunt down Moby-Dick results in the loss of his own life as well as the death of his entire crew (with the exception of Ishmael). Yet Melville's antihero is a metaphor for us all, a warning about what can happen when our quest to realize some inner mission makes us lose control of our individual will—and ourselves.

———

As WE HAVE SEEN, it is when we feel lost that many of the experiences and emotions described in this book can occur. Yet they can also take place in us even when it is someone *else* who is the one who becomes lost. Sometimes our reaction to the plight of another is what catapults us into a state of determination. For as long as there have been armed conflicts, governments and armies have tried to uncover the truth about what happened to those who disappeared as a consequence of them. When soldiers are lost and believed to be captured or in hiding (such as the American fighter pilot who was shot down over Serbia in 1999 during the military campaign there), search-and-rescue teams are often sent in, either to extract the missing individual (as occurred in that case) or to retrieve the body if the person in question turns out to have been killed. I witnessed much of this kind of activity firsthand at Ground Zero a week after the terrorist attack on the World Trade Center. The deep resolve on the faces of the rescue workers, as well as in the eyes of the cadaver dogs, was so intense it was almost palpable.

There has always been a strong religious component behind the impulse to recover bodies, and many people have risked their lives so that the dead could have proper burials. At the national cemetery in Arlington, Virginia, the Tomb of the Unknowns honors those whose identities we will probably never know. Ever since the wars in Korea and Vietnam, where thousands of American servicemen are still listed as "missing in action," whole movements have been built around the search for lost souls. Some (like former presidential candidate Ross Perot) are convinced that many of these individuals are still alive, and their efforts to find them have drawn national attention and surfaced in popular culture through such films as *Missing in Action.*

Yet, sadly, men and women vanish not just in distant lands or as a result of military or terrorist campaigns. They can disappear in our own backyards, in society at large. And some people have made it their life's work to try to search for them. As a chaplain for federal law-enforcement agents, I have spoken with many such individuals and have heard about some of their cases. The agents and officers I serve all have different motivations for and reactions to their work. Some of them are drawn to the investigative aspect of law enforcement, the role of being finders of facts and mystery solvers. Many simply want to help people, either by finding or retrieving a missing person or by catching the criminals responsible for his or her disappearance. Just how an agent responds to the outcome of a particular case depends on how close he or she gets to it.

One FBI veteran, Sam, told me about his first missing-persons case. He was a young special agent just out of the academy in Quantico and was assigned to a violent-crimes squad in a field office in the Midwest. A woman had disappeared from her rural home. There was no note, no blood, no sign of forced entry. Had she been abducted by a stranger? Run off with a secret lover? Been killed by her husband? After hours of interviews with her family, friends, and neighbors, Sam and his fellow agents had come up with nothing. For them, but especially for the woman's loved ones, it was not knowing what had happened to her—the mystery of her disappearance—that was so maddening and painful. In the end, the woman did turn up; she had been kidnapped, raped, and murdered by a drifter (whom they caught) after surprising him as he was burglarizing her home. "The only thing I could take comfort in," Sam said, "was that I'd helped to solve the mystery of what had happened to a missing person, a young wife and mother." He had done his job; he had ended a challenging case and given closure to a family plagued by uncertainty. But he had also been the bearer of profound tragedy and was torn by his twin roles.

Many of the missing persons Sam has searched for have turned out to be runaways (at that point, it is the family and social-service agencies that try to resolve the problem). Others have turned up dead, or were never found at all. Often the bad guys are apprehended; sometimes they're not. In the face of these uncertainties and frustrations, the way Sam has chosen to deal with the feelings he must confront as an FBI agent is to be sympathetic to the people involved in his cases but also to a large extent detached from them. He fears that allowing himself to get too connected to a person or a case could jeopardize his work and imperil his psyche, hurtling his heart and soul into the maelstrom of emotions that the victims themselves are experiencing.

Yet there are times when an agent *does* get connected, when the search affects the searcher in life-altering, sometimes painful ways. Sam's supervisor on the violent-crimes squad, Arnie, was an experienced special agent and a "prototypical tough guy," as Sam described him to me. He was a large, powerfully built man, a Vietnam veteran, and the former SWAT team leader for their field office. ("He would always come to work in cowboy boots," Sam recalled.) Arnie was in his late forties when Sam served in his squad. A few years after the woman's kidnapping and murder, their squad was assigned a case involving a twelve-year-old boy, who had been abducted in broad daylight while he'd been riding his bike with a friend. Arnie, Sam, and the other agents interviewed the boy's friend and a couple of witnesses. They gathered only the most basic pieces of information. An unfamiliar van without license plates had pulled up along the two boys and stopped them. A white male of indeterminate age and of vague description had jumped out of the vehicle, forced the twelve-year-old into it, and then sped away. That was all the squad had to go on. The child had vanished.

"Arnie grew especially attached to the case," Sam recollected. "He was determined to solve it. Arnie had his own twelve-year-old son at home, and he imagined himself in the position of the missing boy's father. He met with the child's family constantly, giving them updates and trying to collect further clues that might help the Bureau with the mystery." Arnie became close to all of the family members. He took on the case as his special mission, personally distributing sketches of the suspect, devoting many hours of his time as well as those of the squad to the investigation, and setting up a command post in a remote area upstate that he visited regularly. Arnie worked on the case for months, even after Sam and the other agents had been assigned to new ones, and after the few leads that they did have had grown cold.

"As time passed," Sam said, "Arnie became melancholy and short-tempered. He couldn't accept the fact that the FBI, with all of its resources, was unable to solve the case, let alone 'save' the boy from whatever fate had befallen him." They never found the missing child. There was no body, no finality, no closure. Arnie's fierce resolve wasn't enough to bring about a happy ending, and he developed an open wound. His job was to solve crimes and catch criminals, and in this case he had done neither. Despite his determination and zeal, he had no real control over the situation. He was frustrated and furious. "I believe that the case wrecked my former squad leader," Sam shared with me, "this tough guy who had at first seemed almost impervious to pain." Arnie was never the same. He soon left the violent-crimes squad and returned to the SWAT team. Eventually he left the Bureau altogether, to lead a much quieter life with his family. Arnie's impassioned search transformed his soul. Whether it made him a better man or a broken one is, at least for Sam, a matter of debate.

———

FOR NIETZSCHE, it is the will to power that represents the most evolved aspect of the human character. It is this quality that allows the truly great individual to stand above the rest of the herd. I have selected the men and women in this chapter, however, because they exhibit not the will to power but the will to *persist.* What they do seem to share with Nietzsche's *Übermenschen* is a profound grasp of the necessity, even spirituality, of affirmation, an understanding that without perseverance, no fear, no hardship, no obstacle can ever be overcome. Our bold determination can rescue us from the most formidable of challenges— or doom us when it mutates into obsession. Some degree of self-confidence is necessary before we embark on a mission to emerge from the maze, and though our first impulse may be a desire to accomplish our goals on our own, we will sometimes need the help of others. More important than self-reliance is a capacity for hope, as well as the ability not to give up but to give over.

SEVEN SURRENDER

Where I am, I don't know, I'll never know, in the silence you don't know, you must go on, I can't go on, I'll go on.

SAMUEL BECKETT, *The Unnamable*

DESPITE OUR BEST EFFORTS to drag ourselves out of the existential wilderness, there are times when it seems as if progress and even movement are impossible. No outburst from our hearts or expression of our will is capable of breaking through a brick wall. One way of responding to those things that limit us is simply to reject them. "Isn't it much better," Dostoyevsky writes, "to recognize the stone walls and the impossibilities for what they are and refuse to accept them if surrendering makes one too sick?" Anyone who has ever experienced adversity, or faced just how limited and vulnerable he or she truly is, understands the appeal of such a position. Who among us wants to concede his or her finitude? But in the end, denial is no answer. And in some respects, the stubborn refusal to surrender is, paradoxically, a sign more of weakness than of strength.

It *is* sometimes possible to penetrate walls, yet not in the ways we ordinarily think. Barriers, constraints, limitations—in short, all those things that we believe impede our advancement as human beings can be, in a spiritual sense, illusions. The contrary is true: Experiences that force us to confront our humanity, with all its fragilities and flaws, can be surprisingly valuable opportunities for personal growth. If we are to grow, however, we must be willing to *give*. The theme of surrender is a dominant one in many of the world's great religions. An individual who practices Islam (an Arabic word that means surrender or submission) is one who bends his will to God's. Similarly, a committed Jew puts on the "yoke" of God's sovereignty (*ol ha-malkhut* in Hebrew), while a devoted Christian imitates Jesus by placing the moral weight of the "cross" upon his or her own shoulders. In the religious context, the transcendence of walls or limitations is contingent on offering a part of ourselves to God—our egos, pride, and false feeling of independence. Spiritual surrender is about not giving up but giving over, about voluntarily relinquishing that which separates us from the divine.

This is a daunting task. It takes enormous effort to be able to let go of such familiar and comfortable aspects of our nature—especially to do it out of conviction rather than as the result of theological or political coercion (as is frequently the case in fundamentalist approaches to religion). Most people are not born with an attitude of surrender. But it can be learned—sometimes as the result of a trial by fire.

Jolene is a single mother and a personal trainer from North Carolina. Several years ago, her daughter (who was five) came home from school very upset. Her class had just been shown a movie on what to do in the event of a house fire. Jolene's daughter remained upset every day for the next week, and kept expressing to her mother how afraid she was that there would be a fire in their own home. One Saturday morning, after a character in a children's television show jumped out of a burning house, Jolene's daughter started crying and again telling her mother how scared she was that something bad was going to happen to them. "At that point," Jolene says, "I started asking myself, 'Is my daughter having a premonition?' And then I started to say, 'If she is having one, please, God, don't let any-thing happen to her.'"

A few months later, following a training session with one of her clients, Jolene had a strange feeling that she should go home. By the time she drove up to her house, smoke was billowing out of the windows. Jolene was able to race inside and save their cat before the fire grew too intense. After the firefighters had put out the blaze and left the scene, Jolene's house was nearly destroyed. Fire, smoke, and water damage had made most of it uninhabit-able. "But from almost the minute this happened," Jolene remem-bers, "I went into this state of 'Thank you.' I just found myself saying 'Thank you' to God—'Thank you for not letting my daughter get hurt.'

"It was bizarre," Jolene continues, "that I didn't really experi-ence any trauma. My heart and mind were filled with gratitude more than anything else. The firefighters said that sometimes people just *know*. But regardless of how we sensed the fire, I felt that the prayer for my daughter had been answered. For the next nine days, until we found a new place to live, we lived in a burned-out house cluttered with debris. I could have gotten upset and angry. I could have waged a war with the flow of life. But I didn't. I surrendered to it." It was that surrender that gave Jolene the strength and the serenity to get though the painful process of making a list of all her lost possessions for the insur-ance company and moving on with her life.

"When you give yourself over to a higher power," Jolene says, "and live in a state of gratefulness, everything changes. In a way, I felt *empowered* by the fire. In its aftermath, I experienced an energy beyond anything I'd ever known. God had responded to my deepest longing." But in the end, it was Jolene who was the one in control: "When something bad occurs in life that you can't do anything about, you are given a choice—you can react angrily, or you can accept it and keep your eyes on your goals and on what is really important to you. Often that's not what you've just lost. For me, surrender is a lot like love. It brings focus, happiness, breath. We all need to breathe. Even our souls need to breathe. And when life whacks you with a disaster, giving yourself over totally to something or someone beyond yourself is the key to breathing, to survival."

Jolene admits that holding onto this attitude isn't easy, that it is an ongoing struggle for her: "When my life feels splintered, when it starts to fray at the edges, it gets very hard to retain my focus and to stay centered. Surrender doesn't just *happen* to us— it's something we have to *work* at. It's an active, creative, powerful experience. And it's an experience that everybody wants. That's the reason people fall in love: We are looking for something to surrender to. We're all seeking food for our souls."

———

THE PROPHET EZEKIEL, like other Jews of his time, was carted off by the Babylonians into exile in 598 B.C.E., and lived with his exiled compatriots along the Chebar River. It is there, a few years later, where the heavens open and he receives his famous and powerful vision of divinity described in the first chapter of the book named after him. It is a vision both celestial and bizarre, filled with winged and four-faced beasts, flaming wheels, images of clouds, ice, and fire, a sapphire throne, and deafening noise. (Some of the early Jewish mystics found in this description of the Divine Chariot the mysteries of the godhead, and developed an esoteric system around it known as Merkavah mysticism.) The vision is so unfathomable and overwhelming that, at the close of the chapter, Ezekiel falls face-down on the ground— an expression of submission as much as confusion.

What the prophet submits to is his humanity in the presence of God's infinity. Ezekiel's behavior is the outer manifestation of his awareness that even a prophet is bound by the limitations of the human mind. Ezekiel, unable (and seemingly unwilling) to try to penetrate the secrets of the Celestial Chariot, instead becomes a passive vessel for the divine message. Like his predecessor Saul and the other ecstatic prophets, Ezekiel gives himself over to—and is possessed by—the transcendent, something that appears to be a prerequisite for receiving and transmitting God's word. Ezekiel recounts this harrowing but transformative moment: "And [God] said to me: 'Son of man, stand upon your feet, that I may speak to you.' Then spirit entered into me when he spoke, and set me upon my feet, and I heard him speak to me." (2:1–2) It is not Ezekiel's will but God's that lifts the prophet from the earth.

Ezekiel receives his prophetic commission in a unique and striking way, one that again utilizes the imagery of submission. God charges Ezekiel: " 'And you, son of man, hear what I say to you: Be not rebellious, like the rebellious house. Open your mouth and eat what I give you.' And I looked, and behold, a hand was stretched out to me, and behold, it held a written scroll. And he spread it before me, and it had writing on the front and on the back, and there were written on it words of lamentation and mourning and woe. And he said to me, 'Son of man, eat this scroll.' So I opened my mouth and he gave me the scroll to eat, and he said to me, 'Son of man, let your body eat and fill your stomach with this scroll that I give you, and go, speak to the house of Israel!' Then I ate it, and it was in my mouth as sweet as honey." (2:8–10, 3:1–3) Though Ezekiel is being "force-fed" the words he is to convey to his sinful people, the prophet's surrender to God's will is a cause not for despair but delight. The mystical scroll becomes a meal for his soul.

One of this story's teachings seems to be that spiritual uplift comes, paradoxically, through surrender. Ezekiel says that after his sacrifice of self, "Spirit lifted me up, and I heard behind me a great noise, as the glory of God arose from its place. But spirit lifted me up and took me away, and I went lifted up in the air and greatly moved in spirit, the hand of God being strong upon me." (3:12–14) Ezekiel, more intensely than any other prophet, finds his spiritual experience claiming and, in a certain respect, controlling his body. He is fully united with the words committed to him, to the extent that they become part of his flesh and blood. And the divine spirit that now resides within Ezekiel literally transports him from place to place throughout the narrative. At one point, the spirit of God carries him aloft and grants him a vision of the temple in Jerusalem, placing Ezekiel "between earth and heaven." (8:3) There, midway between terra firma and terra incognita, the prophet experiences both the terrifying and the elevating dimensions of mystical union.

Though it is through spiritual passivity, or quietism, that the divine spirit enters and animates Ezekiel, it is an emptying of self that Ezekiel *chooses*—and in that respect it is a very active decision. Letting go and allowing himself to become an instrument for God has ambiguous consequences. This "son of man" (God does not refer to Ezekiel by name), being mortal, feels pain as he tries to communicate God's words of castigation to an unrepentant community; he also experiences liberation and even bliss as the burden of independence gives way to a state of integration with the Most High. The relinquishment of self-control in favor of self-surrender is the path of the mystics, and it is not an easy one. But it is a model that has much to teach us as we struggle to find our own way.

The later biblical figure Daniel shares some of the features that make Ezekiel such a powerful spiritual model. Like Ezekiel, Daniel is exiled (under Nebuchadnezzar) to Babylonia. Daniel lives at the royal court and plays a prominent role as an interpreter of dreams and cryptic inscriptions. When a new ruler, Darius, takes over the kingdom, Daniel retains a high post in the court. But the new governors grow jealous of him and convince the king to issue a stern edict: Any person who offers a petition to any god or man other than the king within thirty days will be cast into a den of lions.

After Daniel learns of the decree, he continues to perform his religious obligations as before: "The windows of [Daniel's] room were opened toward Jerusalem, and three times a day he bent his knees and prayed, and gave thanks to God, as he had done earlier." (Daniel 6:11) But suddenly Daniel's enemies burst into his chamber and "catch him in the act" of offering his petitions and supplications to God. They then go to inform on him to the king, telling Darius that Daniel, "who is of the children of the exiles of Judah, pays you no heed, O king, nor the edict you have signed, and prays [to his own God] three times a day." (6:14) The king at first tries to spare Daniel, his trusted advisor, from the gruesome fate that his own edict stipulates, but the conspiring governors publicly remind Darius that even he cannot rescind a royal decree once it has been made. Unwilling to undermine his own authority, Darius orders that the letter of the law be followed and has Daniel cast into a den of lions. Before a stone is placed in front of the mouth of the den, sealing Daniel inside, the king says to him: "The God whom you serve continually—he will deliver you." (6:17)

After a sleepless night, Darius returns to the den and calls out to Daniel: "O Daniel, servant of the living God, has your God been able to deliver you from the lions?" (6:21) Miraculously,

Daniel replies from what should have been his tomb: "My God has sent his angel, and shut the mouths of the lions; they have not harmed me. [God] has found me innocent, and I have done you no wrong." (6:23) Relieved and overjoyed that Daniel has not been killed, the king commands his men to remove the stone and take Daniel out of the den. Not only is he still alive—he emerges completely unscathed. In retribution, the conspirators (along with their wives and children) are then thrown in with the ravenous beasts instead, "and before they reached the bottom of the den, the lions had crushed their bones to pieces." (6:25)

In this story, Daniel displays the phenomenon of self-surrender in several ways. At the outset, he knows that observing his religious practices is going to put him at risk—but he does it anyway. His subservience to a spiritual tradition (for him, it is the will of God) overrides all external factors and allows Daniel to transcend his worldly fears. He is aware of the dangers of such a position, but he is certain that he is doing nothing wrong (in the spiritual sense). Daniel's commitment and conscience make the path he must take clear. Praying on his knees is merely an outer manifestation of the submission to God that occurs in his soul. The narrative itself gives us the reason why Daniel was able to evade the jaws of death—"because he had trusted in his God." (6:24) The implication accords with biblical theology: Had Daniel *not* given over his life to divine providence, the outcome would have been very different indeed.

There are strong thematic echoes of Ezekiel in the book of Daniel. When it comes to imagery, those echoes can become roars. The image of the Celestial Chariot appears again in Daniel chapter 7, and it is strikingly similar to the one in the first chapter of Ezekiel (four unearthly creatures, wheels, a throne, a mysterious human-like figure). Ezekiel has his mystical vision by a river; Daniel's takes place in a dream. But in each man's vision, fire plays a key role. An interesting element in Daniel's portrait of the Divine Chariot (also referred to as the Throne of Glory) is the *Nahar Dinur,* the River of Fire. We learn of an "ancient of days . . . whose garment was white as snow, and the hair of whose head was like pure wool; his throne was fiery flames, its wheels burning fire. A river of fire issued and came forth before him." (7:10) The Jewish mystics held that this holy fire came from the sweat of the creatures that bear the Throne of Glory, and that when our own spiritual practices reach a fever pitch— the result of emotional fervor and religious devotion—our sweaty bodies get bathed in the same fiery, animal energy.

The texts in Ezekiel and Daniel exerted profound influence over Jewish mysticism. But fire is an image of great import to mysticism generally (in the Christian tradition, Mechthild of Magdeburg—to give just one example—writes extensively about sacred fire). Fire represents an intangible but overpowering force, an ungraspable entity that can either comfort or kill us. As a transcendent reality we ignore or defy at our own peril, fire is an effective metaphor for God. The mystics frequently conceive of God as a "consuming fire" (as God is sometimes called in the Bible): To be "eaten" by God through prayer or meditation is to reunite the human soul with its divine Creator. Yet that can happen only when we vacate ourselves of ego. In a related image, we become "chariots" for God when we make room for the divine to dwell within us.

————

ARTISTS, WRITERS, AND COMPOSERS often have a sense that their work is not something they achieve but, instead, *receive*. While mystics describe having their souls infused by the divine spirit, even atheists in the creative fields talk about the mysterious power of the "Muse," the source of their inspiration. Etymologically, "inspiration" means the interiorization of spirit—but for that to occur, we must first surrender to its call. Erich Fromm discusses how the Sabbath embodies that same integration of the material and the spiritual. For Fromm, the Sabbath—perhaps the central institution in biblical religion—is the expression of freedom in its fullest form. Yet it is a freedom rooted in the ideas of giving up and of giving over. In traditional Judaism and Christianity, the Sabbath is a day when we refrain from work. As Fromm writes, "By not working—that is to say, by not participating in the process of natural and social change—man is free from the chains of time, although only for one day a week." The Sabbath is our anticipation of the messianic time, a taste of eternity that only we can allow ourselves to experience.

In Fromm's view of his own Jewish tradition, it is not work that is a supreme value but "rest," the state that has no other purpose than that of being human. Since Fromm was a psychoanalyst, the Sabbath probably seemed to him a wonderful vehicle for self-actualization. And for Abraham Joshua Heschel, an important modern rabbi, the Sabbath is the point of synthesis between the psycho-spiritual *and* the aesthetic. On the Sabbath, we have the potential to become artisans of the soul, to create what he calls "palaces in time." But that spiritual architecture is contingent on our helping to construct it—without its builders doing the work, the palace will never be realized. The paradox is that our "work" and our freedom are the result of simply being. When we dwell in the palace, and allow the palace to dwell in us, we create a harmony of mind and spirit, human and divine. We live in the eternal now.

We can also give ourselves over to dreams. That is what Abby (from chapter 4) did when she surrendered to her heartfelt dream of having a child, despite the fact that everyone around her told her it would be impossible. Or what Danny (from chapter 2) did when he realized that unless he truly submitted to an image of himself as clean and sober he would die. In both cases, it was in letting go of their "reality" and bowing to a vision that on the surface seemed so out of reach that they were ultimately able to break through the barriers that held them back. This is what Ruth does in the Bible when she gives up her Moabite identity (though she is explicitly told by her mother-in-law Naomi not to) and gives herself over to a new one as an Israelite: "Do not ask me to leave you, or to refrain from following you; for wherever you go, I will go, and wherever you lodge, I will lodge. Your people shall be my people, and your God my God. Where you die, I will die, and there will I be buried." (Ruth 1:16–17)

———————

I NEVER KNEW MY GREAT-UNCLE DAVID very well. He lived in Dallas, and I grew up in Chicago, so our paths crossed only a couple of times at family gatherings while I was a child. But I had heard that he had been in combat as a tank commander during the D-Day invasion in France, and I always had an almost mythic image of him as a fighter. When I was older, we finally had a few real conversations, mainly about his wartime experiences, but also about Judaism—he and my great-aunt Charlotte had strong religious identities and were active in the Dallas Jewish community. To me, David was one of those archetypal figures from what Tom Brokaw calls "the greatest generation." We had our last actual conversation while I was in Dallas for a conference. By that point, David was an old man. He had a serious heart condition and was very ill. The condition had been with him for a long time, and my parents had said for several years that he could succumb to it at any moment, but he somehow kept hanging on. As usual, he was humble and stoic. He was far more interested in talking about Middle East politics and Jewish beliefs than discussing his heart problems.

After the conference, I returned to New York City and began my career as a young rabbi. David watched my rabbinate unfold with genuine interest, always asking my parents what new position I had taken up and what new book I was working on. He even read most of my work. Some years passed. David's health deteriorated. My parents gave me updates on his condition, and I spoke with Charlotte on occasion over the telephone to find out how David was doing. When I got the chance to travel again to Dallas to follow and write a magazine article on a professional storm chaser, I went first to visit my great-uncle. Charlotte welcomed me into their home and led me to the bedroom. David was there, along with a nurse. He was lying on a cot, and there were tubes attached to his body. He was near death. I said hello, but David didn't seem to recognize me and couldn't speak in any case. He slipped in and out of consciousness, and he was in great pain. At times David would be curled in a fetal position. When he moved, he let out a moan that chilled me to the bone.

I sat with Charlotte in the kitchen. She told me that David's death was no longer a matter of weeks or even days away but of hours or minutes. She didn't cry. "I've been getting myself ready for this for years," she said in her southern drawl. It was clear how much she loved him, but it was also clear that she knew there was nothing more she—or anyone—could do for David now. "He's in so much pain," she said. "I just want him to let go and let it end." It suddenly struck me that, though I was David's great-nephew, I was also an ordained member of the clergy. Rabbis, ministers, and priests often lose sight of (or feel ambivalent about) their clerical roles when they are in the presence of their families (and it is easier to fall back into more comfortable roles as nephews, nieces, sons, and daughters). But I felt that, at this point, Niles the rabbi might be of more help to David than Niles the great-nephew. I suggested to Charlotte that I pray with him.

I walked back into the bedroom and stood over David. This figure who in so many ways had seemed larger than life to me now looked so small. His limbs were thin and frail, and he was moaning. His right leg hung off the side of the cot, and he appeared as if he already had one foot in the grave. David had always come across as so grounded, so rooted in reality. Yet now his appearance was ethereal. The roots that had held him down over the years were now being extracted from the world, one by one, before my eyes.

I put my hand on David's leg. He gazed up at me with a kind of vague recognition, then looked away toward my great-aunt. I decided to recite the *Sh'ma,* one of Judaism's most important prayers, with him and for him. It is a statement of religious belief that is traditionally said on one's deathbed: *Sh'ma Yisrael Adonai Eloheinu Adonai echad* ("Hear O Israel, Adonai is our God, Adonai is one"). David again gazed at me. I'm not certain that he knew who I was, or that he really understood the words I uttered, but in his glance I felt that something was being exchanged between us.

Less than an hour later, I received a telephone call from Charlotte at the place I was staying. She informed me that David had died. I told her how sorry I was, how great a man I thought David had been. Charlotte said she was convinced that on some level David grasped the words I had recited, that saying the *Sh'ma* had helped him to let go, to give up his long fight. To me, however, David was still a warrior. But what I witnessed was a different kind of heroism: the heroism of surrender. David hadn't given up. He had instead chosen to give *over* his soul to God—on his own terms, and in his own way. I am a firm theist, but I am not a big believer in supernatural phenomena. Yet I couldn't help feeling that, somehow, there was a deep, mysterious link between that prayer and my great-uncle's relinquishment of his life. As Jung writes, "'Physical' is not the only criterion of truth: There are also *psychic* truths which can neither be explained, proved, nor contested in any physical way."

One of the things that most struck me about David's death was that it seemed more an affirmation than a negation of his life. It was not a suicide, a fatal assault on one's own being. David didn't take his life. He *gave* it. Suicide is a false kind of surrender, a rejection—not a reluctant relinquishment—of the gift of life that is grounded in despair or mental illness. Surrender at its deeper, more spiritual level involves no such negativity. It is a loving attempt to unite with God and, when death is imminent, to do it in an absolute and purely non-material way. That final exertion requires a detachment from the world of the living. There may be, as some have noted, a connection between an ecstatic experience of divine unity and a wish for death (to make the temporary merger permanent), but an acknowledgment of the temptation to end our lives before all the anxieties, sorrows, and trials intrude once again is sufficient expression. In the words of Kohelet, "For everything there is a season, a time for every experience under heaven." (3:1)

———

ONE BIBLICAL FIGURE who slams head on into the brick wall of existential uncertainty is Job. The book of Job has been treated by many as perhaps *the* quintessential account of one human

being's pained attempt to fathom the reasons for his suffering—
and, by extension, the mysteries of God's ways. It is a tale in
which an innocent man is subjected to the worst and seemingly
most senseless kinds of torture as he serves as a pawn in a contest between God and Satan. The book—a collection of dramatic
scenes, dialogues, speeches, and theophanies—raises the perplexing and ultimate questions of divine justice (theodicy) and
the meaning and purpose of life.

The narrative begins with a session of the divine assembly,
during which God calls Satan's attention to Job's exemplary
piety and moral character. Satan questions how "pure" Job's motivations really are and suggests that without all of his material
blessings (Job is a wealthy man), he would curse God to God's
face. Satan's implicit wager is accepted by God, who grants Satan
permission to test Job by any means except an attack on his person. What follows is a demolition of Job's property and family: A
Sabean raiding party takes away Job's oxen and asses and slaugh-
ters his servants; a fire from heaven consumes his sheep as well
as other servants; three bands of Chaldeans steal Job's camels and
slay yet more servants; as Job's children attend a feast at the
home of his oldest son, a violent desert wind destroys the house,
crushing everyone inside. But instead of cursing God after these
horrific calamities (as Satan had predicted), Job blesses God, and
accepts his lot with resignation: "Then Job rose and tore his robe
and shaved his head. He fell on the ground, and worshipped. He
said: 'Naked I came from my mother's womb, and naked shall I
return there. God gave, God took away; blessed be the name of
God.'" (1:20–21)

At the next session of the celestial assembly, God taunts Satan
for having failed to break Job's steadfastness to his Creator. Satan
replies that Job has not truly been tested, since the restrictions

that God placed on the initial trial prevented any harm from coming to Job personally: "All that a man has he will give for his life. Reach out and strike him, touch his bone and flesh, and he will curse you to your face." (2:4–5) Reacting once more to Satan's implied challenge, God permits him to test Job further, with only a single stipulation—Satan may not take Job's life. Satan leaves his audience with God and proceeds to afflict Job with a terrible disease. The malady causes Job such misery that he scrapes himself with a potsherd while sitting in ashes. Job's wife urges him to curse God and die, but Job—at least at first— reaffirms his submission to divine sovereignty and upbraids her for her foolish words: "Shall we accept good from God, and not accept evil?" (2:10)

Three of Job's friends (Eliphaz, Bildad, and Zophar) hear of his latest calamity and travel to console him. Seeing Job from a distance, they barely recognize him. The men, appalled by their friend's physical appearance and personal tragedy, sit on the ground in silence with the anguished Job for seven days and seven nights. It is after this period that Job's quiet resignation reaches its breaking point. He cries out with a bitter complaint: "Job opened his mouth and cursed his day. Job spoke out and said: 'Damn the day I was born, the night that said, "A boy is begot." That day—let it be darkness. . . . Why did I not die at birth, emerge from the womb and expire? Like a stillbirth would I were hidden, like babes that never saw light. Why did knees receive me, or breasts give me suck? For now would I be lying quiet.'" (3:1–4, 11–13) The voice of surrender has become a voice of protest, one that belongs to a man who wishes he had never been born and who now yearns for release through death.

Job questions the reason for existence in the face of life's miseries: "Why gives he light to the wretched, life to the bitter of soul, who yearn in vain for death, seek it like a treasure-trove, glad to get to the grave, happy to find the tomb? To a man whose way is hidden, whom God has fenced about? Instead of my food come sighs, groans are poured me as water. What I most feared has befallen me, what I dreaded has overtaken me. I have no rest, no quiet, no repose, but continual agony." (3:20–26) Clearly, Job is not depicted here as a person who has serenely accepted his fate. Whatever expressions of resignation he demonstrated earlier in the narrative have been replaced with those of indignation. Job implies he is a person who cannot find his way, a kind of caged animal. And he shows that the journey between surrender and defiance is an ongoing and fluid one, dependent on the interplay of circumstance, attitude, and faith.

The following thirty-three chapters contain debates and dialogues between Job and his three friends, as well as a series of speeches by a young newcomer named Elihu. The goals of all four of Job's companions are similar: to argue that God is just, that there is meaning behind Job's misfortunes, that Job is not as pure and guiltless as he tries to make himself out to be. In his final speech, Elihu states that God's power and providence are simply beyond human understanding. God created snow, rain, thunder, lightning—can Job comprehend, much less create, such things? Then God enters the picture, and the debate, directly. God speaks to Job out of a whirlwind, questioning how someone so limited in knowledge could challenge the divine plan. God asks Job, "Where were you when I laid the foundations of the earth? Tell me, if you know so much." (38:4) What does Job know of the taming of the great oceans and the ordering of the constellations? Can Job provide food for the lion, or domesticate the wild bull? Is it by Job's wisdom that the hawk soars? All of these features of nature are, ultimately, the products of a divine mind.

It is not a beautiful rainbow or a gentle brook but a raging maelstrom out of which God addresses Job. This is an awesome and ominous image, one that communicates the generative and annihilative capacities of a powerful storm as well as, by implication, the multivalent (and sometimes contradictory) dimensions of God. The whirlwind suggests that God does not just have ambiguous qualities—God is ambiguity *itself.* Confronted with this fathomless mystery, what else can Job do but surrender to it? In 40:4, Job says, "Lo, I am of small account—how can I answer you? My hand I lay on my mouth." In *Answer to Job,* Jung writes that "in the immediate presence of the infinite power of creation, this is the only possible answer for a witness who is still trembling in every limb with the terror of almost total annihilation." But Job does not die. God is a Creator as much as a Destroyer. Jung continues: "Yahweh is not split but is an *antimony*—a totality of inner opposites—and this is the indispensable condition for his tremendous dynamism, his omniscience and omnipotence."

God speaks to Job from the whirlwind once again, this time utilizing not natural but *super*natural images to stress the fact that there is an unbridgeable gulf that separates the divine and the human, in terms of both intellect and ability. God asks Job to consider two mythical, primeval beasts, Behemoth and Leviathan. God tells Job:

> "Behold now Behemoth which I made as well as you. . . . His bones are tubes of bronze, his gristles like iron bars. He is a primordial production of God. . . . Who would grasp him by his eyes? Pierce his nose with barbs?" (40:15, 18-19, 24)

Following this description of the great land monster, God has Job ponder the monster of the sea:

"Can you draw out Leviathan with a hook, press down his tongue with a cord? . . . Will you fill his hide with harpoons, his head with fishing spears? . . . Who could confront him unscathed, under the whole heaven, who? . . . From his throat coals glow, flame pours out his mouth. . . . Iron he regards as straw, bronze as rotten wood. No arrow can put him to flight; slingstones change to chaff on him. . . . On earth is not his equal." (41:1, 7, 11, 21, 27–28, 33)

No human being could have given birth to these mythic beasts—and no human can ever hope to control them. In the rabbinic tradition, Behemoth and Leviathan figure prominently not just in prehistory but also in the messianic era. These monsters represent the seething, underground (or, in Jung's words, unconscious) forces that are a perpetual threat to the cosmic order. Only God can conquer such powers, and in a final apocalyptic battle, God—who was responsible for creating the two beasts—slays them. In the age of redemption that follows (according to one of many legends that involve these creatures), the righteous, sheltered from the elements beneath the skin of Leviathan, feast on the flesh of Behemoth.

In some homes, this divine drama is enacted every week. There is a custom (based on a reference to Leviathan in Psalm 74) among some Jewish communities of eating fish heads on the Sabbath. When I was the guest of honor at my Israeli friend Igal's home, what I think was the head of a large carp was placed in front of me one Sabbath dinner as my special "treat" (though I wasn't sure what part of it I was supposed to eat). If the Sabbath is our foretaste of the messianic age, then this strange custom certainly conveys the same ideas about the ultimate triumph of order over chaos, joy over fear, life over death. It also conveys the idea that our struggle with those forces must be engaged in not just at the End of Days but throughout our lives. Yet without God, without an acceptance of divine sovereignty and an acknowledgment of our place in the universe, we will not find redemption. This is the truth that Job finally submits to when, after the second theophany, he says, "I had heard of you by hearsay, but now my own eye has seen you; I recant and repent in dust and ashes." (42:5–6) In the end, God triumphs over Satan, and Job, his fortune restored and with a new family, lives out his days in peace.

Like the firestorm atop Mount Sinai, the maelstrom in the book of Job serves as the site of divine revelations, startling and life-altering disclosures of ultimate truth. But whether it is a storm or a sea serpent (or, as we saw in the books of Ezekiel and Daniel, fiery chariots or thrones), the use of imagery to impart divine knowledge is a vital part of biblical spirituality. For human beings, a firm understanding of God is as elusive as the wind. How can words describe that which is beyond linguistic expression? Tangible images, like works of art, offer an alternative way of trying to comprehend—or at least experience—a transcendent reality that defies comprehension. But even images are imperfect. For that reason, and because it is so closely connected to the act of surrender, some religious thinkers believe that *silence* is perhaps the best form of spiritual expression we have.

––––––

KIERKEGAARD SAYS that faith necessitates our making a leap into uncertainty and a willingness to adhere to an attitude of infinite resignation about our ability to fathom the radical mystery of God. In the spiritual context, surrender thus becomes something that is far more active than passive. Fromm, as a psycho-analyst and non-mystic, calls this having the "x attitude." He argues that irrespective of whether there is a God, such an attitude can be of enormous benefit to us, for it produces "a letting go of one's 'ego,' one's greed, and with it, of one's fears; a giving up the wish to hold onto the 'ego' as if it were an indestructible, separate entity; a making oneself empty in order to be able to fill oneself with the world, to respond to it, to become one with it, to love it. To make oneself empty does not express passivity but *openness*."

True freedom is not about having the ability to choose between multiple options but about bringing one's will into alignment with the will of God. This may seem counterintuitive, yet even with all the new "freedoms" that the last century has given us (quick and easy divorces, Internet access, dozens of different brands of shampoo), happiness still seems as rare a human commodity as ever. It is when we give over, when our goals and desires mesh with and become indistinguishable from those of the divine harmony, that life takes on a more liberating and fulfilling dimension. Letting go of our preoccupation with self can feel like experiencing a little death, but what we gain in return is a deeper sense of direction and a new, more meaningful life.

EMERGENCE

Anything can happen to anybody at any time. That is one of the built-in features of human life (and, for some, a lamentable one). Even if we have worked hard and had our share of luck, there are no sure things, no certain outcomes that flow from our experiences. Accepting our limitations and giving ourselves over to uncertainty seem to be the penultimate steps in our attempts to make it out of the wilderness. But what happens when we do? Where do we emerge when we reach the other side? Much of that depends on context and receptivity, on what circumstances present themselves and on how open we are to encountering them. Yet while we will all live out our own destinies, the end result is not always evident to us when it comes to the fate of others.

Nathan, another great-uncle of mine, is a man I never knew at all. But my Hebrew name, *Natan,* is his name, and I have always felt a special affinity for him. Nathan was born in 1909. He was a peasant who worked on a Jewish collective farm somewhere in the Ukraine. Nathan was tall, slim, and smart, and at the time of the Second World War he had a wife named Manya and one child. He had been drafted by the Red Army at the age of nineteen and had served for three years. Nathan was called back into it in 1939 and probably saw combat during the war between the Soviets and Finland. He returned to his family for only a very short period of time: In 1941 he was drafted once more to fight against the Germans. No one ever saw him again.

That is everything I know about Nathan's life. As I have grown older and become more interested in my family history, I've wanted to learn the truth about what happened to him. At times I've tried to visualize various scenarios, placing myself on the opposite end of a movie camera that was pointed directly at him.

SCENE 1: *His fingers numb from the frigid winter, Nathan lifts his rifle and aims over the trench at the German troops positioned in the woods. He pulls the trigger repeatedly. Fury fills his heart. These are the bastards who are murdering his family, his people. Suddenly there is a deafening boom that shakes the ground. Nathan feels a piercing, hot pain in his back. He is now looking up at the gray sky. He can't breathe. In his peripheral vision, he sees other soldiers racing around frantically. Then the motion of the soldiers seems to slow down. The dim light darkens.*

SCENE 2: *It's been weeks, and his fever is no lower. The veins in Nathan's head feel as if they're going to explode. A nurse wearing a mask that covers her mouth walks up to his cot occasionally to take his temperature or to offer him something to drink. The purple rashes that envelop his body burn intensely, but he doesn't have the strength to scratch them anymore. The field hospital smells of disease and death. He hears the sounds of the front in the distance, muffled by the tent's canvas. Another corpse is taken out for burial. Nathan waits.*

SCENE 3: *Soon after their capture by the Germans, Nathan and the other Jewish soldiers are separated from the rest of their battalion and forced to march for days without food or water. During one brief stop, Nathan drinks from a filthy puddle on the side of the road before a guard kicks him in his ribs and orders him back in line. The march ends at a rural train station, and the men are crammed into boxcars. The next morning, the train slows and screeches to a halt. They hear large dogs barking outside. Through a tiny slit near the top of his boxcar, Nathan can make out three stubby smokestacks.*

SCENE 4: *It would be so simple. He is young and strong, and the border is only three kilometers from their position. All he'd have to do is sneak away from his unit late at night and evade a couple of his own sentries. How many more miserable years are they going to make him give his life to the army? How can he take care of his wife and child on a peasant's meager wages? The burdens feel unbearable. There is a whole world waiting for him to explore beyond the pain and poverty Nathan has known. With a single decision, he could set himself free. It is just a matter of will.*

I will probably never know how, when, or where Nathan was lost. Any of these (or other) scenarios seem plausible to me. Most likely, he perished sometime between 1941 and 1945, when the war ended. He would have been my age now. But he could have survived and constructed a new life for himself. For all I know, he is a very old man living somewhere in the former Soviet Union right now. What is certain is that, however Nathan's life played out, he would have had no family to return to—his wife and child were killed at some point during the war. For me, just the knowledge that Nathan exists, or rather that the mystery of his life exists, has affected me in profound ways. It has given me a better perspective on my family's background and a deeper appreciation of my own lot. It has given me a direct experience of how extreme life's uncertainties and ambiguities can really be. And it has given me a personal myth, an almost mystical link to a soul that helps to ground mine. In an age of detachment from the past and of disconnectedness from each other, Nathan is one of the roots that secures me to flesh-and-blood reality.

———

IT IS AFTER WE ACCEPT MYSTERY AND PARADOX that we can move past them. The book of Ecclesiastes begins with the author (who is a member of Israel's elite society) expressing dismay and outrage at the fact that rich and poor, saint and sinner, sage and fool all share the same end. "How can the wise man die like the fool?" Kohelet asks, recounting his reflections of earlier years. "And so I hated life, because all the work done beneath the sun seemed worthless to me; for all is vanity and a striving after wind." (2:16–17) With time and perspective, Kohelet extricates himself from his anger. By the end of the book, he seems more comfortable with the contradictions in human life. "Of making many books there is no end," Kohelet states, "and much study is a weariness of the flesh." (12:12) Our limited knowledge is not enough to penetrate the mysteries of the universe. Acceptance of uncertainty is a far better strategy for living than is the useless resistance to it.

There are times when we move not only from one attitude to another but from one place to another. As the people of Israel are pinned against the shore of the Reed Sea by Pharaoh's army, they fall into a state of crisis. Before them is an impassable body of water, behind them vengeful soldiers and charioteers. Their fear, as well as their indecision about what to do, is understandable. God instructs Moses to tell them to "journey forward." (Exodus 14:15) It is only when the Israelites take the first step, when they make a willful leap into the unknown, that God intervenes in the dire situation. A miracle occurs. In a scene dramatized on film by Charlton Heston and Cecil B. DeMille, "Moses held out his arm over the sea and the Lord drove back the sea with a strong east wind all that night, and turned the sea into dry ground. The waters were split, and the Israelites went into the sea on dry ground, the waters forming a wall for them on their right and on their left." (14:21–22) God helps the Israelites further by disorienting the minds of the Egyptians (still in pursuit of the former slaves), who start to panic and retreat. After the people of Israel have emerged onto solid ground, the waters collapse, drowning Pharaoh's troops.

What follows Israel's passage from confusion to hope, from death to life, is a song, a joyful, collective expression of triumph and thanksgiving. When this "Song at the Sea" is read in synagogue, it is customary for the whole congregation to stand throughout its recitation. The only other scriptural reading that receives this mark of special respect is that of the Ten Commandments. The song extols God's power and reflects the Israelites' reverence and gratitude for it:

> I will sing to the Lord, for he is highly exalted;
> Horse and driver he has hurled into the sea.
> The Lord is my strength and song;
> He is become my salvation;
> This is my God and I will enshrine him;
> The God of my father, and I will exalt him. . . .
> Who is like you, O Lord, among the celestials;
> Who is like you, majestic in holiness,
> Awesome in splendor, working wonders? (15:1–2, 11)

The song also describes Israel's unfolding desert pilgrimage, its transition from one stage in its sacred journey to the next. After depicting the enemies in Israel's path, the song continues:

Terror and dread descend upon them;
Through the might of your arm they are still as stone—
Till your people cross over, O Lord,
Till your people cross over whom you have ransomed.
You will bring them and plant them in your own mountain,
The place you made to dwell in, O Lord,
The sanctuary, O Lord, which your hands established.
The Lord will reign forever and ever! (15:16–18)

Some thinkers interpret biblical images of water and land as representations of inner states. In Psalm 69, water functions as a metaphor for the psalmist's feeling that he is drowning; in the book of Jonah, the prophet is spit onto "dry land" after he has worked through his own angst and been in essence "baptized" under the sea. The passage of the Israelites from the Reed Sea, to dry land, to the holy mountain is a similar journey from crisis to emergence.

At the close of the collective song, the prophetess Miriam takes a timbrel in her hand and, with the other women, leads a dance and a chant of celebration. This spontaneous expression of joy is their response to the physical and emotional shift that has taken place in their community and their lives. It represents an epiphany of sorts, an awareness that—with God's help—they have confronted hardship and peril and made it through the experience not just intact but victorious. According to a Jewish mystical tradition, a person who recites the Song at the Sea "audibly and joyously" (Miriam sings a refrain from it in 15:21) is pardoned for his or her sins. What this teaching implies is that the appreciation and affirmation of our lives, and of God's role in them, is all we need to redeem our souls. Miriam's example of how to act at the end of an arduous journey ought to be a model for us today, especially in an era when such public displays of happiness and exuberance are all too rare.

Yet joy is not and cannot be a constant human state. Miriam's journey, like all our journeys, continues. In the very next verse, the people of Israel find themselves in the wilderness of Shur, thirsty and anxious. Their struggle to reach the Promised Land has not ended—they will wander in the desert for many years to come. The Israelites will get lost, they will reorient themselves, then they will become lost again. Their odyssey through the wilderness is a mirror for the way many of us perceive our own lives. But we should not view that inherent tension as anything negative. It is reality. Human life is punctuated by semicolons, not periods; it is an ongoing, staggered process of fits and starts. Put much more beautifully by T. S. Eliot:

> "What we call the beginning is often the end
> And to make an end is to make a beginning.
> The end is where we start from."

—————

MARLENE IS A MUSICIAN from Florida. She projects the interior calm of someone who has weathered an emotional storm. "I was held hostage by my love for my father," she says. Marlene and her father had been very attached to one another over the years. They had an unusually close relationship, made all the more intimate following the premature deaths of her only two siblings. When Marlene's mother died, her father was devastated. His relationship with Marlene was not enough to prevent him from spiraling into despair. He was an old man by that point, and in the painful aftermath of his wife's death, he was in a very fragile and vulnerable state.

Marlene's father had moderate dementia, something that had been with him before her mother's death. "Even with his condition," she says, "he still knew that he wanted to have a last chapter. He was a charismatic man who had great charm and great wealth, and he wanted—no, he *needed*—a replacement for my mother. He was filled with denial—about aging, about the loss of his powers, about the death of his wife. My father was ripe for the picking—and he got bagged." While Marlene had been aware that her father had begun dating someone three weeks after the funeral, it was only after she had gone out of town for work and tried to reach him over the telephone that she knew he had become a target. "I couldn't get through," she recounts. "I called him all night, but the line was always busy. I knew he'd been speaking a lot with the woman—who was twenty years younger than him and had a reputation as a manipulator and a gold digger—but to be on the phone like that told me she'd already made my father a mark."

Although Marlene tried to get her father to wait just six months, until the unveiling of her mother's gravestone, he married the woman ten weeks after they'd met. During the two-year period that followed, Marlene felt as if she had lost her father (to her wicked "stepmonster," as she called the woman). As the sole surviving heir to her father's fortune, Marlene had expected to be provided for by his inheritance as she grew older, and had made personal and professional plans with her husband with that in mind. With the stepmonster now in the picture, everything changed. The savings accounts were gradually but inexorably depleted. Older, frailer, and more fearful, Marlene's father became more concerned about losing his new wife than losing his daughter and, under the firm guidance of the stepmonster, rewrote his will so that she became the exclusive heir.

"I felt completely betrayed," Marlene remembers. "I felt a blinding anger and hurt. I moved between rage and pain, and there was no release anywhere. I confronted my dad about it, about feeling not only betrayed but *abandoned* by him. I wanted his attention and love again far more than I wanted anything else from him. It didn't help. So it was either back into analysis or try something else." Even though it was difficult for her, Marlene chose to surrender to the situation and, in the face of negation, perform an act of affirmation. She decided to plant a garden. "At that point," she says, "I didn't give a shit about ambition or about my troubles—I just wanted to float and create and survive." The garden became Marlene's wellspring of vitality and peace.

Less than two years later, Marlene's father was on his death-bed, and she was by his side. It was an experience that perma-nently altered her view of him—and of herself. "I returned to my father," she says, "but I didn't return to the same relationship with him. Even in his haze, we were both more honest with each other. We saw one another's naked need. Before, he and I had idealized each other and then become angry with those idealiza-tions when they let us down. In that hospital room, we forgave one another. And I realized that my father didn't have to be mythic to be worthy."

Marlene had further insights. "I came to terms with my own selfishness," she says, "about his love and his money. I gave up pursuit of the inheritance in order to get what was *really* impor-tant to me: our relationship. I wanted to ease his way. It stopped being about me and instead became about him, about giving him a peaceful journey. I became the person I wanted to be. I mourned for the father I thought I had while he was alive. By the time he was near death, there was almost nothing left of him. The step-monster had sucked him dry and didn't want anything more to do with him. In the end, he was mine. He was in my arms when he left this world, and he left it peacefully—God had provided me with a gift. My father had given himself to me. I could feel his pulse as it twitched on the top of his head. He let go of life like a fluttering little bird."

Marlene learned to let go of something as well—her desire for perfection. "Now I have total acceptance," she says. "I rarely experience anger or sorrow. I have a new perspective and a new inner direction. There are only a few things that are ultimately important in this world. But it took the trauma of the episode with my father to reveal that basic truth to me. And to give me a revitalized and more hopeful life."

———

A PRIMARY LESSON OF THE STORIES IN THIS BOOK is that we can progress from being lost at one stage in our lives to finding hope and renewal at another. We can *evolve*—though that evolution involves struggle. Freud thought that struggle was at the heart of human nature. He argued that the conflict took place between our instinct for life and our instinct for death, between the id, ego, and superego, between the conscious and the unconscious. For Erik Erikson, one of Freud's disciples, our conflicts do not occur in a vacuum but, rather, with other people and the outside world. In Erikson's psychoanalytic model, each of the eight stages of human development is marked by a crisis, or turning point. We can either master the developmental challenge or fail to resolve the core struggle.

If we deal successfully with life's existential conflicts (such as identity versus role confusion, or intimacy versus isolation), we evolve as human beings; if we fail to work through them, we stagnate. There is a continuity in human development, and this continuity is reflected in the stages of growth: Each stage is related to and affected by the others. In chapter 3, Mara and Brian described how their struggles with loneliness led to a changed worldview and a fresh approach to living. Mara's isolation resulted in stronger connections with other people and trust in the power of redemption. Brian's seclusion catalyzed feelings of humility and compassion of which the sculptor had been unaware. "I emerged from my depression with serious battle scars," he says. "I felt like Moby-Dick at the end of the novel, bloody and bedraggled with old harpoons, lances, and ropes. But I did break free. I did make it out alive."

When we examined Jacob in chapter 1, the biblical patriarch is a confused man whose famous "ladder" dream helps to reorient his soul. The dream is a powerful epiphany that affects the way Jacob views the world, but it does not lead to a clear transformation of character, an evolution not only of his perception but of his person. The event is an important step in his spiritual growth, as well as toward reconciliation with his brother Esau. Before that can happen, however, Jacob has a second, more challenging (even terrifying) nighttime encounter.

In Genesis chapter 32, Jacob's long exile is drawing to a close. It has been twenty years since the young Jacob tricked Esau into giving him his birthright, and it is time for the patriarch to face his past before he can proceed with his future. Jacob sends messengers to make contact with his older brother and to assess Esau's position regarding their relationship. When the messengers return, they inform Jacob, much to his distress, that Esau is on his way to meet him—along with four hundred of his men. In a defensive measure, Jacob divides his people into two camps. He asks God for protection. He offers a potpourri of livestock to Esau as a present. Then he waits.

That night, Jacob rises and sends his family and their possessions across the Jabbok River. He is left alone. And there, by the
banks of the Jabbok, Jacob wrestles with a mysterious figure
until daybreak: "When [the figure] saw that he had not prevailed
against [Jacob], he wrenched Jacob's hip at its socket, so that the
socket of his hip was strained as he wrestled with him. Then he
said, 'Let me go, for dawn is breaking.' But [Jacob] answered, 'I
will not let you go, unless you bless me.' The other said, 'What
is your name?' He replied, 'Jacob.' He said, 'Your name shall no
longer be Jacob, but Israel, for you have striven with beings
divine and human, and have prevailed.'" (32:26–29)

There are many different interpretations of both the nature
of this encounter and the identity of the mysterious stranger.
Maimonides thought the experience was a prophetic vision. Some
commentators view the adversary as Esau's guardian angel, out
for vengeance. Psychologists have seen the stranger as a projection of Jacob's own inner demons, or his conscience, at last calling him to account. But whatever it is that happens, and whoever
it is who confronts Jacob in the middle of the night, the experience transforms his soul. When a person goes through a name
change in the Torah (such as Abram becoming Abraham, or Sarai
becoming Sarah), it frequently indicates a change in character.
Like a new king ascending a throne, Jacob receives a name that
indicates he is ready to assume his inheritance and take on the
mantle of moral leadership.

At dawn, the patriarch limps away from the scene of the confrontation. Jacob has been seriously injured. He sees Esau and his
four hundred men coming toward him, and the intent of his
older brother seems clear. But Esau, prepared to meet (and react
to) the sibling he remembers from his youth, the one who
cheated him out of his birthright and tore apart their family, sees

a very different Jacob hobbling toward him. For the patriarch has emerged from his murky struggle as not just a new man but a humbled one. Jacob bows low before Esau seven times. He asks forgiveness from his brother, if not in words, then through appearance and manner. What Esau beholds is not a deceitful, arrogant Jacob but a wiser, repentant *Israel,* a man now more deserving of the love of a long-lost brother than a violent death by the sword. The two men run up to each other and embrace. Esau kisses Jacob/Israel on the neck. Both of them weep.

Jacob pays a price for his struggle. Still, even with his war wounds, he is depicted as triumphant, transformed by his experience in character and in attitude. Moses, another great patriarch, undergoes a similar transformation. The first time we see him in the Torah, Moses kills a man. Though the person is an abusive Egyptian taskmaster, it is an action that forces Moses to flee into the desert. Wherever this killing stands on the plane of morality, many of the rabbis believed it is what keeps Moses from entering the Promised Land many years later. At a minimum, his action displays a violent anger that is just below the surface and that will erupt on other occasions. Thomas Mann offers a psychological deconstruction of Moses' personality: "His birth was disorderly. Therefore he passionately loved order, the immutable, the bidden, and the forbidden. Early he killed in frenzy; therefore he knew better than the inexperienced that, though killing is delectable, having killed is detestable; he knew you should not kill."

Moses does not personally kill again. But his temper expresses itself in other ways. While he is communing with God on Mount Sinai, Moses' people, unable or unwilling to wait for his return with the sacred covenant, conspire with Aaron to create and then worship a golden calf. Moses catches them in the act: "As soon as

Moses came near the camp and saw the calf and the dancing, he became enraged; and he hurled the tablets from his hands and shattered them at the foot of the mountain. He took the calf that they had made and burnt it; he ground it to powder and strewed it upon the water and so made the Israelites drink it." (Exodus 32:19–20) As bad as the behavior of the Israelites was, to deliberately destroy the word of God—*in God's very presence!*— seems like a clear and audacious act of sacrilege, unacceptable for a prophetic leader. For this reason, some of the rabbis claimed (quite imaginatively) that, as Moses approached the camp, the letters of the Ten Commandments lifted from the tablets and flew back to God; as a result, the stones became too heavy for Moses and he dropped them.

Most sages, however, did not absolve Moses for his deed and acknowledged that he had trouble controlling his emotions. Like the rest of us, Moses was a flawed human being with problematic aspects to his personality. After he shatters the tablets, Moses has the golden calf melted and pulverized, and forces the Israelites to swallow the gold dust to which they had prayed earlier. His actions appear to be more the expressions of his turbulent passions than detached and punitive judgments. In addition to his anger, Moses also shows a propensity toward isolation, possibly even a degree of misanthropy. There are several instances in the Bible (such as Exodus 24:18 and 34:3–4) where he severs contact with the community he is supposed to be leading and goes off alone into the mountains for long periods of time. When he does communicate with his people, the mountaintop recluse demonstrates an authoritarian style of leadership. He doesn't nurture or comfort—he gives orders. Perhaps that is why in Exodus 32:1 the Israelites refer to him as "that man."

Yet Moses matures with age. His character evolves. After

decades of wandering in the wilderness, Moses emerges from the Exodus experience as a person who exhibits deep compassion and love for his people. Near the end of the book of Deuteronomy, Moses addresses his community and his successor. He is now an old man. God has already told him that he will not be allowed to cross the Jordan with his people. But Moses consoles and reassures them: "The Lord your God himself will cross over at your head; and he will wipe out those nations from your path and you shall dispossess them. . . . Be strong and of good courage, be not in fear or in dread of them; for the Lord your God himself marches with you: He will not fail you or forsake you." (31:3, 6) Though he stands at the cusp of the Promised Land, aware it is a place he will never enter himself, Moses focuses not on his own disappointment but on the concerns and anxieties of those he serves.

Moses does not leave the Israelites without a new leader to take his place. He calls Joshua to stand before the entire community and says for all to hear, "Be strong of good courage, for it is you who shall go with this people into the land that the Lord swore to their fathers to give them, and it is you who shall apportion it to them. And the Lord himself will go before you. He will be with you; he will not fail you or forsake you. Fear not and be not dismayed!" (31:7–8) Far from being an angry, uncaring, or jealous person, the Moses we see here is a man whose personality and attitude have been transformed by time and experience. He has mellowed over time, and his actions reveal someone capable of a fellowship and a serenity of soul that did not seem possible in him during his younger years.

At the conclusion of the Torah, Moses ascends Mount Nebo and gazes (longingly?) over the great land he cannot set foot on. According to the text, he meets his death with silence and in peace. But in one midrashic legend, Moses resists. After learning he is to die, he draws a small circle around himself and tells God that he will not take another step unless God annuls the decree. Moses prays, pleas, begs not to be taken from the world. Even his soul implores God not to be removed from the great prophet's body. Yet finally, following loving and reassuring words from his Creator, God kisses Moses—a kiss that draws his spirit from this world to the next. In reaching his end, Moses has found a new beginning.

———

IT WAS NEAR DUSK when I took the ferry across the Daintree River to Cape Tribulation. My summer adventure in northern Australia was half over. The last week or so had involved a variety of activities, from bungee jumping, to horseback riding, to scuba diving along the Great Barrier Reef. On the previous evening in the area, I'd taken a boat ride along the Daintree, an ancient waterway that separates tropical north Queensland from a region that contains some of the most primitive, unusual, and dangerous plants and animals on earth. As the small boat traversed the river and its tributaries, fruit bats the size of terriers flapped their hulking wings overhead. The eyes of crocodiles, made blood red by the beam of light that was aimed at them, blinked on and off at me in the distance.

My timing was terrible. I was driving deep into a remote place that had very few services, and in addition to the problem of hiking in diminishing sunlight through dense and unfamiliar forest, my return trip would take place in almost total darkness on a rough and winding road. If my headlights died, I'd have to spend the night in my car. But I couldn't wait. I had to head to Port Douglas the next morning, and this was my only opportunity to explore one of Australia's most exotic parks. My journey into the jungle got off to a rocky start when I demolished my rearview mirror. As a virgin to left-side driving, I'd gotten too close to a tree.

After crossing the river, I felt as if I'd entered a different world. Scientists believe that the Daintree region is a remnant of the original rainforests of Gondwanaland, the primeval landmass from which the Australian continent slid south 135 million years ago. (Similar traces of those early rainforests have been found in Antarctica as well.) What preserved the unique, pristine habitat of the Daintree was the fact that it was able to survive the last ice age (because of its southern latitude). In some ways, the Daintree offers a glimpse of life before humans—or at least of a time before human dominance. Many of the bizarre creatures in the area pose a mortal threat to human beings. Aside from the crocodiles and pythons hiding in the swamps, creeks, and mangroves, even the ostrich-like cassowary, with its razor-sharp talons, can eviscerate a person.

Cape Tribulation, my destination, was at the northern tip of Daintree National Park. The sun was setting as I pulled over my car and hiked into the bush. Although a narrow trail led to the beach, I was acutely aware of—and at times heard—the otherworldly beasts that lurked in the shadows around me. I grew scared as with each step the forest darkened. I wondered how far off the ocean was, how black the bush would be when I tried to make my way back out. I walked faster. Then, after what seemed like an interminable amount of time, the sounds of invisible animals were replaced by the sounds of an invisible sea and sky. Suddenly I could see through the tops of the trees, through the vines and canopies that had shut out all else just moments before. And then, abruptly, the rainforest ended, and I emerged onto Cape

Tribulation's beach. My face was slapped by a cool wind that rustled on through the woods. Before me was the Coral Sea, part of the South Pacific and extending into infinity; the water appeared purple, and at the horizon the deepening blue sky could barely be distinguished from the sea. Behind me was a wall of coastal rainforest that sheltered a universe of stunning (and startling) flora and fauna.

I was standing at the intersection of two ecosystems, two entirely different spheres of creation. And it wasn't merely the surface appearances of these worlds that were so remarkable— it was what they contained within. Only a few days earlier, I had been underwater, scuba diving southeast of Cape Tribulation. The Great Barrier Reef (which stretches along practically the whole of Queensland's eastern flank) was only a few miles from the beach. I'd seen firsthand the caverns and ramparts of coral, the anemones, the sharks, the schools of rainbow-colored fish. I knew what was down there, swimming and swarming beneath the purple sheath. I also knew what was inside the forest wall, the tropical wilderness of kookaburras and kingfishers, wombats and wallabies. I'd observed their strange forms and listened to their haunting cries.

A thin band of white sand was all that separated the rainforest from the reef. These extreme contrasts, and my position between the two, reminded me of the time I stood at Icy Reef. Yet there was a profound difference. At Icy Reef, the predominant feeling that I experienced was that of tension. It was an episode that led to disorientation and confusion, to a sensation of being lost. At Cape Tribulation, it was not bewilderment but *serenity* that seemed to grip my soul. Maybe it was because some time had passed since I'd been in Alaska, and I was open to a new perspective. Maybe it was because I'd worked for the prior two years as a congregational rabbi and was more at peace with myself and with human life. Whatever the reason, the contrasts that had at first seemed perplexing and potentially destructive now felt right and good. The poles that had seemed incongruous and oppositional now felt like necessary components of an interlocking unity. My feeling of tension had given way to one of harmony. Heraclitus put it best: "The cosmos works by harmony of tensions, like the lyre and bow."

Nothing had changed in the external world—all that had shifted was my perception, my perspective on life. Developing the capacity to view existence as a context for hope rather than despair, as a place of abundance rather than of absence, is a cause for profound gratitude. I did not have a partner, family, or community to mark the occasion with me, but I did have a spiritual tradition to keep me company. I recited a Jewish prayer, the *Shehecheyanu:* "Blessed are you, Adonai, sovereign of the world, who has enlivened us, sustained us, and brought us to this moment." It was getting too dark to remain any longer. But I didn't want to go. I didn't want the feeling to stop—a feeling that wasn't exactly joy or happiness but, rather, acceptance. It was more than a surrender to the cosmic forces yet less than a complete embrace of them. Perhaps that too would come in time. Still, I had rarely known such inner equanimity before.

Why leave a transcendent experience of deep serenity and reenter the dark forest? Why go back the way I came? The footpath I had to walk on might have been the same, but my relationship *to* it had been forever changed. I could take this memory with me, this transformation within that would necessarily alter my interactions with the world without. After absorbing the knowledge that by becoming a different person I was entering a different world, I peeled myself away from the beach, hiked through the bush to my car, and drove into the heavy, expanding night. When I took the ferry across the Daintree again, I left not only Cape Tribulation but a vision of a primeval Eden that instilled in me new faith in the human ability to find a more tranquil home in the midst of the perplexities and vicissitudes of life.

———

THERE IS A STORY in the Talmud about four sages who enter a place called Pardes ("Paradise"), often understood as a metaphor for transcendent experience. Only one of them, Rabbi Akiva, survives the event unscathed. Aher becomes a heretic, Ben Zoma goes insane, and Ben Azzai dies. Their encounter with transcendence is bewildering and traumatic, and each of them responds to it (and was probably prepared for it) in a different way. Like the sages, all of us emerge from our brushes with mystery in different and unpredictable ways, depending on who we are and on what we are able to receive. Some of us are wounded in the process; some enter a new domain of hope and promise. The tribulations (and periodic crises) of human life—the dark events that force us to face our weaknesses and limitations—can be valuable catalysts for growth or barriers that paralyze us. While we can't prevent them from occurring, we *do* hold the power to direct and utilize their energy, allowing us to sometimes refresh and reorient our souls.

CONCLUSION

I am circling around God, around the ancient tower,
and I have been circling for a thousand years,
and I still don't know if I am a falcon, or a storm,
or a great song.

RAINER MARIA RILKE,
A Book for the Hours of Prayer

ALTHOUGH WE DO NOT ALL EXPERIENCE EACH STAGE examined in this book, every human being feels lost at certain points during the course of his or her life. The best way to overcome that feeling is not to deny or sidestep it but to confront it head on. There is a lot we can learn from our bewilderment, but in order to learn from it we must first acknowledge it, even embrace it. There are no magic bullets to erase the discomfort and pain that such an experience brings with it. What is necessary are strength, courage, and, perhaps most of all, stamina. In the end, it is its capacity to endure that may be one of the greatest assets of the human soul.

Allowing ourselves to feel helpless, like the dogs in Martin Seligman's experiment, will lead only to despair. Instead, we must make leaps of faith, not just once or twice in our lives but every day. By viewing confusion as a catalyst for transformation and renewal, by possessing the hope that every difficult episode will be transient, that within it lies the potential power for inner growth, we will emerge as humbler, wiser men and women.

Thomas Aquinas claimed that ceaseless bliss was not possible in this life—only in the life to come. Mortality is a process of being lost, then found, then lost, then found again. It is a wandering in the wilderness that continues until our death.

Human life is an *adventure* in the most profound and literal meaning of the word: a daring undertaking that involves unknown risks and hazards. One of those hazards is the internal anarchy that is born of our confusion. Yet as Nietzsche writes, it is only when we have chaos within ourselves that it becomes possible "to give birth to a dancing star." Whether it is making a desert journey or producing a dancing star, it is critical for our psycho-spiritual development that there be a mythic dimension to our lives. Some of those myths might be collective ones, such as the Israelites' crossing of the Reed Sea or Washington's crossing of the Delaware. But some must be personal. Those myths will be different for each of us, shaped and individualized by our own struggles and stories. All of us have dragons to slay. All of us have worlds to create.

Existence is not a rigid dichotomy, but an indistinct blending, of light and darkness. These two (mythic and metaphorical) powers are not discrete but intertwined; they are engaged not in a war but a dance. There are traces of darkness within every burst of light—and sparks of light inside every eruption of dark-ness. When I consume the head of "Leviathan" at Sabbath dinner, I am dramatizing our triumph over, yet also *absorption of,* the shadow. As Heraclitus said long ago, "Out of life comes death and out of death life, out of the young the old and out of the old the young, out of waking sleep and out of sleep waking, the stream of creation and dissolution never stops."

With the passage of time and the gift of perspective, our experiences of being lost often become something else, something palatable. It is then that we realize how those disturbing events or periods were rooted not in actually *being* lost but in *feeling* lost. Perplexity and pain are subjective experiences. The degree to which we feel them, if we feel them at all, depends on who we are and where we are in our lives. Because we are always in the middle of them, we do not usually see our lives as part of a larger pattern or trajectory. Yet much of our worldview, as well as our sense of ourselves, relates directly to our perception of reality. A young man or woman in agony over the loss of a first love, for instance, may in later years become extremely grateful that the relationship came to an end when it did. Whether or not we are lost hinges on our perspective and perception, and together they can make the difference between living a life suffused with negativity or with hope.

One way of illustrating this idea is by examining a figure-ground diagram:

Which is the principal figure and which is the background? Is the image above that of an upside-down bat, or of Batman? Are we looking at a picture of a creature of the night or of the Caped Crusader? The answer, of course, is both. How we view this diagram is contingent on who we are and what we allow ourselves to see. But as the Kotsker Rebbe said, the person who does not see God everywhere will not see God anywhere. On the mystical level, darkness and light are not separate realities but interconnected components of a cosmic whole. Learning to view all our experiences as necessary elements in this spiritual unity, regardless of how pleasant or unpleasant they are, is the key to a tranquil soul.

About a week or so after the collapse of the World Trade Center, I walked through Ground Zero. It was during the Days of Awe. Before me was utter devastation: a wasteland of smashed buildings and shattered windows; hideous, fantastic pillars of twisted steel; plumes of smoke rising eerily from the rubble. As a law-enforcement chaplain, I talked to cops, firefighters, and rescue workers from dozens of agencies and cities. I remember one K-9 unit, a sheriff's deputy and his dog. Even though by that point all they were pulling out were bodies, his retriever wouldn't let him sleep. Everyone there, whether human or animal, was focused on their work, on trying to serve. I was moved by the acts of commitment and expressions of love that permeated that hellish place. And I was astounded by the vision of so many people finding their deepest, most beautiful selves in the heart of such an immense void.

Martin Buber defines a miracle as an event that instills us with a feeling of "abiding astonishment." The experience of being lost is the shadow side of experiencing something miraculous: Both are bewildering, both transformative. Over time, if we are sensitive and perceptive, we will come to view *all* of life with a sense not of shock but of wonder. With wisdom, we will shed our doubts and fears, regardless of the challenges or hardships we must confront. We will welcome the adventure. For it is life itself, with all its ambiguity and mystery, that is the hidden miracle—overlooked, omnipresent, waiting to be discovered and explored.

Acknowledgments

I AM DEEPLY GRATEFUL to those individuals who opened their hearts to me and shared some very difficult experiences from their lives as I interviewed them for this book. Though their names have been changed, they know who they are, and they have my most profound thanks. I also thank my parents for giving me the foundation in my religious tradition that has allowed me to appreciate as well as to access the sacred stories about the biblical men and women from which I have drawn. And I thank my ancestors for preserving and transmitting a spiritual heritage that has faced obstacles, and even hostility, for too many centuries.

Holly Gewandter and Ellen Gould, co-founders of The New Shul, are close friends, allies, and intellectual sparring partners. My relationships with them have been among the most significant in my life, and I am grateful to them for making me their rabbi and helping me to live a dream. I take none of it for granted. I thank the Shasha family for allowing me (temporarily) to turn their beautiful mountaintop home in Oregon into a writer's retreat, and Sylvia Stein and Mark Philips for the gift of a laptop computer to use while I have been on the road and technical assistance when I need it—which, unfortunately for them, is often.

Alison Granucci, Michael Craft, and the rest of the faculty, staff, and students at the Omega Institute have helped me to grow as a teacher and a human being. Raquel Sanchez, Marilyn Perlman, and Jennifer Abadi have given me much-appreciated insights and advice for this book. Carolyn Hessel, executive director of the Jewish Book Council, has been extremely supportive of my writing career. As always, my literary agent, Ellen Geiger, has guided me diligently through the publishing process and given me greatly needed counsel. I want to thank most of all my friend and editor Toinette Lippe, and the team at Bell Tower. This is the second book I have written under Toinette's watch, and she remains a wonder to me, someone who is as reliable and steadfast as she is talented. Toinette is more than an editor. She is a teacher.

May this book help others to find their way.

ABOUT THE AUTHOR

NILES ELLIOT GOLDSTEIN is the founding rabbi of The New Shul in Greenwich Village, New York. He lectures widely on Jewish mysticism and spirituality and has taught at New York University and the Hebrew Union College–Jewish Institute of Religion. Goldstein is the National Jewish Chaplain for the Federal Law Enforcement Officers Association and was the voice behind "Ask the Rabbi" on the Microsoft Network. His essays and poetry have appeared in *Newsweek,* the *Los Angeles Times,* and many other publications, and he is the author or editor of five previous books, *God at the Edge: Searching for the Divine in Uncomfortable and Unexpected Places; Spiritual Manifestos: Visions for Renewed Religious Life in America from Young Spiritual Leaders of Many Faiths; Duties of the Soul: The Role of Commandments in Liberal Judaism; Judaism and Spiritual Ethics;* and *Forests of the Night: The Fear of God in Early Hasidic Thought.*